I0437995

Travels With Mi Sang

Travels With Mi Sang

MILDRED MAYLEA MCBRIDE

Copyright © 2009 by Mildred Maylea McBride.

ISBN: Softcover   978-1-4363-8982-2

All rights reserved. No part of this book may be reproduced or transmitted in any
form or by any means, electronic or mechanical, including photocopying, recording,
or by any information storage and retrieval system, without permission in writing
from the copyright owner.

This book was printed in the United States of America.

To order additional copies of this book, contact:
Xlibris Corporation
1-888-795-4274
www.Xlibris.com
Orders@Xlibris.com
27546

Dedicated to one of our great traveling companions, Ruth C. Wetzell who put up with and loved a rascally little girl.

PAK, MI SANG

MI SANG PAK was a child I had seen a picture of at a service at the Nazarene church in Honolulu. A group of Korean children were singing and my friend Cathi Jones and I had gone to find a child to support. Mi Sang with friends in orphanage in Masan. Korea

Her little worried face made me know she was the one who needed my help, so I signed up to support her. The group caring for these children was "Compassion". They had several orphanages in Korea and she was in one of them. Mi Sang IN Love Valley Orphanage in Korea

We were required to send $21.00 a month and that would be enough to care for the little girl. (N0, it was not!) Cathi chose a child and we were on our way. Mi Sang was three at the time, the picture had been taken when she was six months old and had just been brought to the orphanage by her aunt, I learned later.

I decided a year or so later that I wanted to adopt her if that was possible. We found out soon after that "Compassion" did not want their children to be adopted. It just happened when Mi Sang was five Ruth Wetzel and I had taken a course from the University of Hawaii that took us to five Asian countries to learn what we could about each country in five days time. The last country we would study would be South Korea. I had permission to visit with her, Ruth must have had it too because we saw the city, with Miss Ko and Mi Sang. Mi Sang visiting Ruth and Me in Seoul, Korea

The Honolulu group all got to see her and fell in love with her, not that she thought we were so great. We had those great big noses, and were that strange color, and so tall, etc. We took her all around the city and got to know her a little. It made me even more anxious to take her home with me. We were given a marvelous interpreter from "Compassion", Miss Ko, and she was able to help her understand us and us to get to know her. Miss Ko reported Mi Sang's reaction to the things she was doing to the Compassion Main office and Mi Sang herself impressed the man in charge how much a little stimulation could do for a child.

Mi Sang with Miss Ko, our Compassion interpreter Mi Sang with me in Seoul.

It would take five more years to actually get her to Honolulu. I had offered to send money to have her tutored in English but no one could be bothered. I suspected it was beyond them to find someone to do it. I had hoped Miss Ko would take in on. She had disappeared as mysteriously as she had appeared just when we needed her most.

But finally all these years later we had gotten to this point where we were looking for Mi Sang to come through the gates and come home with me.

Mi sang meets Charlie, a friendly black cat of our;

Having her as my daughter was as wonderful as I had imagined, and as frustrating as others had known. She had never been disciplined and she was not about to begin at age ten. Avis Nakamoto brought some Korea girls to help with the language, and one of their mothers was wonderful since she was willing to be on the end of the telephone whenever Mi Sang needed to tell me something. I owed a lot to all of them.

The U.S. Government had caused me the most trouble, I was a single woman therefore must have had some kind of ulterior motive to want to do this. Their conclusion was that I really wanted a maid! I am afraid it was the other way around for many years.

When the news came that Mi Sang was ready to come to Honolulu, it seemed almost too good to be true. This had been such a long wait for her and for me. It was now March 1976, and I had started this in 1970.

First Korea found reasons as to why it could not happen. North Korea was taunting South Korea with the thought that they were selling their children.

Then the United States had problems with her coming into the country. It was all my fault I was single and so probably I had wanted a maid and thought this would be an easy way to get one. Often the U.S. government has trouble making any sense but this was the most ridiculous yet. She was nine years old!

We had gotten all that sorted out and so she was to come. She had been sent to Seoul to stay with a Korean family and "learn about American ways". What she had done there for a month was carry their baby on her back. This did not seem as presumptive to her as it did to me! (Who wanted a maid?)

I had offered to go for her, but they said she would be able to travel alone. So they had dressed her in all the clothes she owned beginning with a set of flannel pajamas, and layered the rest all the way up. The poor kid was in misery, of course. I had said buy and send NO woolen clothes, that we lived in a warm place, Hawaii. NO matter, it was heavy flannel and wool that she had on.

Mi Sang upon her arrival in Honolulu wrapped in wool after a 36 hour flight/

She had been on the plane for many hours, (I believe 36 hours) the plane had gone to Japan, then Hong Kong or some place and finally to Honolulu.

Many people had come along to meet her. Luree and I were at one International entrance, Donna was at another, and Genny at the third. We waited and we waited.

Finally a stewardess came to Donna's door with a hot little girl. Donna motioned to me to come, Mi Sang had shaken her head when she saw Donna there, but Donna was sure it was Mi Sang. I ran over and she smiled and told the stewardess that I was her new mother.

Everyone gathered around and I suppose scared the poor child to death but we hoped she felt welcomed. This was the first arrival of a child adopted from the Asian countries at Harris Church, many more came later. I appreciated so much their love and interest. There were many leis and I guess they made her even hotter. They all realized she was terribly tired even if she was excited, and needed to get home.

We went our way and Luree and I immediately began to take off the heavy jacket, the long sleeved blouse and the woolen pants. She was still covered completely – there was some kind of layer on over the flannel pajamas. We stopped at Chun Hoon's drug store and went in to find a pair of go-aheads and then got rid of the heavy shoes and socks.

We got home to Nuuanu soon and it was cool and pleasant there. A dog and cat met her and she immediately related to them. I took her into the bathroom and showed her the bathtub and she smiled and agreed that would be a good thing. She had loved her baths in Seoul five years earlier.

A dog some cats had greeted her when we arrived at 3194 Alika Avenue in Honolulu, and she had immediately taken to them.

I hope I had given her a good drink of water before that!

Luree left us and I found the lovely clothes that the women of Harris church had given me for her. She chose the coolest looking ones and got into them after the bath.

I showed her the house and yard and soon Avis Nakamoto arrived with some Korean girls who could talk to her. They were high school students and they were in Avis' art class. That was wonderful.

One of their mothers had agreed to speak to her via telephone whenever she could not make me understand what she needed. The girl taught her the telephone number and showed her how to use the phone and they called the nice lady. She was told to call whenever she wanted to talk to some one in Korean. The girls came and took her to a carnival the next weekend and she loved that.

I hope I made some kind of effort to thank them for their great help to her and to me. I was so overwhelmed for the next few weeks that I probably did nothing about it at all.

I had no time off from my job at Pearl Harbor at all so it was necessary to get her enrolled in Nuuanu School as soon as possible. She had had no experience with a school situation at all so we were fortunate to have her put into a class with two wonderful teachers. However, it was March 25th and the year was about over.

As long as she had them – the rest of that school year – things went well, after that the entire thing fell apart. Mi Sang on her way to school at Nuuanu.

Mi Sang on her way to School

First birthday in Honolulu, October 5

Mi Sang praying, she did this often, for every meal and every night.

Mi Sang at prayer in our Kitchen in Honolulu

When school was out for both of us, we went to the U.S. Mainland so she could meet her new relatives and my other friends. That plane trip was not bad at all and we stopped in St. Louis to see Dwight, Sandy and Meredith. we visit with Dwight's family

with the McBrides in Missouri

Mi Sang with violin lessons from Donna De Neeve

King St Honolulu. The adoption papers are signed

1st Halloween "Cinderella"

"Sleep over party"

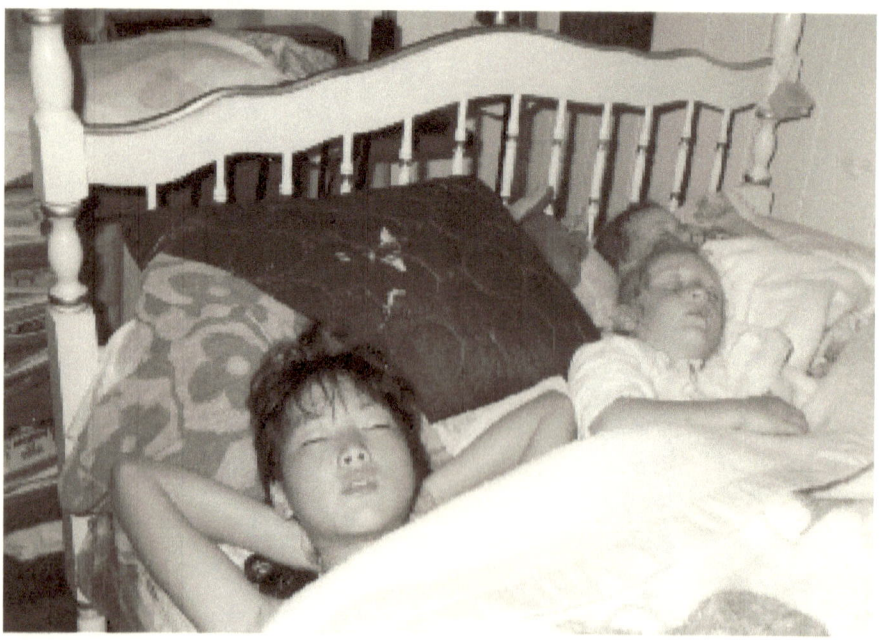

Erica
Kiyosaki
&
Mi Sang
Christmas

Aunt Luree
Hays and
Mi Sang
have some
ice cream.

Walking our Terries

Dwight, Sandy, Meredith & Dione visit us.

Dione, Meredith & Mi Sang in the Hot Tub

In the "Children's Chorus"

Dione McBride
3 years old

Meredith & Dione & Mi Sang Mcbride

Fun in the sand.

She related to Meredith and we went everywhere where little girls would have fun. They did and even the hot, hot days were good ones. I still appreciate all the time Sandy took to let them get acquainted and have us feel good with them all.

We went on to Pittsburgh and Bob and Lib were very nice to her. We went to an empty lot in Wilkinsburg where a small carnival had been set up. There was only one ride, as I remember and it was some kind of one that went on and on. Since he had no business at the moment, it was dinnertime, he was good to us and gave us a long, long ride. Mi Sang was in her glory and I thought it would never end.

Bob drove us to Ohio and we stayed with Pearl and Ernie and visited around the countryside for a week. We three walked all over the farm, and the weeds were away over Mi Sang's head so Bob picked her up and carried her so she would be able to see "our farm". Everyone was very nice to her and I appreciated all their kindness. I think Mary Helen came for us but before that happened, Smithy and Jane Smith, from Monterey, California, arrived at the Ernie Bower farm looking for me and wanting to meet Mi Sang. They had been in Athens, Ohio, Jane had relatives there and they both had graduated from that University. I must have told them when I would be in Ohio and so they came to see us. I did appreciate that so very much. Mi Sang in Ohio.) the Smiths, at the Bower home, etc.

We went to stay with Mary Helen over the weekend, Margaret Riffile came to see us there and that was another nice thing. Mary Helen took us to Cleveland to see Norine and I think we met Jean Hess. These were all college friends of mine and they had families and knew about little girls. We stayed only a little while there and then we went back to Pittsburgh and took a Greyhound bus to St. Louis where Dwight met us and took us back to their house for a few days before we left for Honolulu and school. (Uncles, Dwight and Bob, (Aunt Sandy, Meredith,) dinner in St. Charles Mo. 7

I felt so blessed that I had such nice friends and family who were mostly willing to help a little girl feel accepted and part of my family. I told the Conotton people later that I appreciated their kindness so very much. Pearl told me. "Of course they would love her, she was a dear child." And so she was, and it also was hard for Mi Sang to always know what was expected in this new and strange culture.

Mi Sang entertained Mary Helen and me when we were riding in the car by singing familiar hymns in Korean. We sometimes joined her in English and she was surprised that we knew them.

The Nazarene church in America had sponsored the orphanages and the children did attend church every Sunday and were taught the songs there, I suppose. Likely that was their only experience in a gathering and it was the highlight of their week, she seemed to know some of the Bible stories as well as the songs. She was then and has always been very religious. prayer

The next year in school was very bad for Mi Sang and I did not know a thing about it since she could not tell me anything yet. Finally one of the girls in her class told me how badly the teacher was treating her. She had been put in a corner and the teacher told her that since she could not speak English she was too STUPID to be in her class, she only taught the gifted!

I asked the principal what could be done about the situation. He couldn't think of a thing, the lady in question was such a GOOD teacher. She had tenure so there was nothing to be done.

Genny Wakayama had retired as the principal from a school in the Central District and she volunteered to come and take her out of the class and tutor her. They worked together for some time, unfortunately Mi Sang considered Genny her good friend and she saw no reason to work under those circumstances. "Sesame Street and Mr. Rogers" were getting her English under control and she was learning how things were done in America so we all survived. I was trying too hard to get something that she really liked to do. She became a good swimmer. Donna wanted to give her violin lessons and we tried that. She again tried to not pay attention since it was an auntie who was teaching her. violin lesson)

She made a good friend during that Erica and Mi Sang year at school, who remains a good friend. Erica Kiyosaki Murphy. Erica had a hearing problem so she was having a hard time too.

The year got over and we had a nice summer ahead so we hoped she would be in a better class situation when we returned.

This was her second summer and Mi Sang and I had arranged a freighter trip with Ruth Wetzel and Janet MacCammon. We were to leave from New Orleans, cross the Atlantic and travel around the Mediterranean and eight weeks later arrive back to Houston.

Ruth was my usual good traveling companion and Janet had been with me on the freighter trip to Australia. Of course they were not used to a rascally little girl! (Mi Sang on the bridge, throwing a bottle overboard)

Luckily we got off at each stop and hurried around for the sightseeing so they did get a respite once in a while.

Our first stop in Italy was Livorna, the port for Pisa. Ruth, Mi Sang and Janet climbed the tower. I had found we could take a train to Florence, have time to see some things there and then go on to where the ship was docked, unloading. We would need to find a taxi to get to the ship but they assured me we could. Pisa, ship

We were cutting it a little short so we dashed around looking as quickly as we could and saw much in the time we had. We saw the Baptistery Doors, with the marvelously vivid Biblical scenes, the wonderful bridge over the Arno, the beautiful dormo built with the lovely ice cream colors,(pink, green, blue) David (without his clothes on) according to Mi Sang. She evidently didn't think he should be standing in the square like that. I can't remember if we had time to eat or not, likely we had something, or we would have heard about it.

Everything worked out well; we made the train, found the taxi and got to the ship. We dashed on and the men were obviously relieved. So was I.

We sailed past the volcano "Stromboli" and it was erupting. I asked the steward to ask Mi Sang to leave her hair dressing and come to see it. She was working on the chief engineer's non-existent hair.

We had nearly passed the volcano and it wasn't much anyway, she obviously felt it had not been worth her time, and she hurried back to her work on the hair. It wasn't much of an eruption I had to admit.

We came to the Messina strait and Sicily was glowing with all kinds of lights and colors. I wondered if it might be Mount Etna erupting, but it was the farmers burning their fields for the next year.

The next few days were at sea and were lovely. We were scheduled to go to Thesselaniki, Greece. When we arrived we saw many white tents everywhere. It seemed there had been a very bad earthquake a few days earlier and there was not one safe building in the town. Most buildings were now piles of stone. The people were issued a tent by the government and were to stay in them until their homes could be fixed.

We four wanted to go to a hotel or restaurant to try really good Greek food. The ship unloaded flour all day and all night, so the people had some food if there was a good place to store it that was still standing.

My main thought was for all those 59 tunnels on the train line that we would be taking to Athens the next day. There had been many after shocks so we hoped for the best.

The train traveled above a flat, flat plain below, far below. I thought I knew how that plain got there. We passed Mount Olympus and I thought about all the gods and goddesses living above us.

We would be in Athens for a week taking as many local tours as possible. Then Ruth, Mi Sang and I would fly to Cairo and after our time together in Athens, Janet would go to Rome to camp out and visit as much as she could. In Greece

By this time Mi Sang had had it. We found a hotel in the center of town and the four of us had one room. I hoped Ruth and Janet would not throttle her. We could not eat at our usual time – on ship that was five o'clock – and that suited Mi Sang fine. The rest of us liked it too, but the Greeks eat at 10:00,PM, or later. I like to picnic if things are not better than that, but Ruth does not like to picnic so that would not work. Mi Sang was not willing to compromise or anything, she became a Holy Terror.

Janet left for Rome. I hoped it was not earlier than she had planned. She had her bed, her food, clothes and tent on her back so she was off. I learned later that it all worked out well and she had enjoyed Rome very much.

We took a bottle of water for Mi Sang and walked all around Athens. It was dreadfully hot and that bottle of water was our salvation.

Our first exciting trip was to the Parthenon. We wanted to get in all the main sights before we needed to fly to Cairo to find where the ship would be unloading. The Parthenon had been used as storage for munitions and accidentally blown up in the early 1800's. It had not been hurt enough to keep the magnificent lines from showing what a marvelous building it really was. The muses were under wrap as they were being repaired.

The most difficult thing for the adults was to stay vertical. The entire Acropolis is slippery marble and it is impossible to keep standing unless you were ten and part mountain goat. Mi Sang was flying all around with no problem at all. Ruth and I were just able to keep standing, and I was glad to get down without any broken arms or legs.

The lights playing on the Acropolis after dark made it all the more glamorous. It was as magnificent as I had always imagined it would be. All the broken pieces were concealed and it seemed to be as it must have looked 2000 years ago.

We went to Delphi and listened for the Oracle. She did not speak to us, and we may have been glad not to know what was immediately ahead of us.

We stopped at a beach at Neaplonia and Mi Sang met a little Greek girl and they had a lovely time playing in the water. I keep wishing we could take her around Greece with us but it was not to be.

We went to see "Medea" in the real Greek theater, the same that had been in use some 2000 years ago. We could hear every word. The acoustics were wonderful and the seats were as hard as they had ever been. It was a thrill to hear the same play that the Greeks had heard in the same place some 2000 years earlier.

We saw Marathon, the grave of Agamemnon, and the Strait of Corinth. We visited the agora where St. Paul preached so many years ago. These were all ruins, of course, but it was very real as to what had been there.

The rest of our time in Athens was spent in wandering along the streets and avenues that were so familiar through our ancient history courses.

Mi Sang loved the Greek soldiers guarding the palace in their little "skirts". They were shorter than the kilts in Scotland.

Greece is a hot place and in order to keep the poor child human I insisted that she carry her water bottle everywhere. Food was our biggest problem, when we could get it, it was delicious.

The time came when we needed to leave Greece and get to Egypt. The ship was scheduled to be in Alexandria, so we would fly to Cairo and take the train or bus to Alexandria.

We asked about a room in Cairo while we were at the travel agent. She told us there was no way we could get a room in Greece for Egypt. The agent in Cairo would offer you a lovely room in the city with a bath, that would turn out to be, when you arrived at that address, an empty lot. They were absolutely unscrupulous.

She told us there were kiosks at the airport that would have rooms that we could take a taxi to after we arrived.

We had a lovely flight on a Swiss Air plane. Sitting next to me was a young man who had been working on some business all during our short flight. Not until the lights of Cairo were in view did he speak to us and asked me where we were going to stay.

I told him the story that the travel agent had told us and that she suggested we get a room after we arrived.

He was aghast, and then he said he was sure she was right but that I could not take a child into Cairo at 10:00 at night without a place to stay. He would be getting a car that his company provided for him and he would take us with him to his Swiss hotel in Giza.

When I saw the chaos that was the airport of Cairo, I knew he was right. Somehow I felt we could trust him, and off he went to get the car.

It was now 11:00 PM and the traffic was wild. I must say Eric could hold his own. He was young and he understood the Egyptian mind. He had little use for most of them. Red lights were fair game; the horn was the most used part of the automobile. Each one went his own way, declaring loudly that he must be first. It was almost as chaotic as the airport had been. There seemed not to be any rhyme or reason to the streets and the Nile was always in our way.

About an hour later we arrived at the hotel. It was lovely and very Swiss, so clean and well kept. He did not ask, he told them to find a room for us that the child was very tired and we needed to get her to bed.

They grumbled but they found a room and we thankfully did as he suggested and got ourselves to a shower and bed.

Eric would be gone to work by the time we woke up but he would see us when he came home, he told us. The pyramids were right close and we should visit them and get Mi Sang on a camel.

On Royal Princess - at the canal

We gratefully thanked him and went to bed.

The next morning after breakfast we walked over to the pyramids and were immediately accosted by the Camel drivers. They are a wild noisy bunch and soon one took Mi Sang's hand and led her to a camel. Ruth and I were assigned a funny little cart.

I protested, since I had hoped to ride a camel and I think Ruth did too, but he would have none of it, we were to take that cart! As it turned out that was a very good thing!

The camel drivers are utterly unscrupulous but Mi Sang seemed to be having a good time so we sat in that thing and waited for her. Ruth got out to take a picture of her on the camel and was backing up to get a good shot, when she fell off a four foot ledge that was invisible in the sand.

At the same moment, the camel, with Mi Sang on, took it upon himself to run off. Mi Sang told me many years later that the camel driver dropped the rope and the camel left, and that she was scared to death. Ruth had twisted her knee badly and could hardly stand. The camel driver came to assist Ruth and left Mi Sang and the camel to themselves. I started after them, and for some reason the camel stopped. He must have thought better of his fling and he waited until another camel driver lifted Mi Sang off. She may have remembered that she had been scared, but at that moment she was beaming! Mi Sang on the camel

We went back to the carriage and we were very glad to have it since Ruth could not walk. We went to the hotel still a little shaken by the turn of events. Mi Sang had seemed to have loved the whole thing and didn't seem a bit worried.

We paid the lot (they screamed and yelled but we stuck to our guns and went on our way) and Ruth limped in the direct of our room at the hotel. When we got there we found our luggage in the hall and the door locked. We were told that our room had been reserved and that we were to go to an Arab hotel that was near by. We protested but no one listened to us.

I suppose they took us to the new place. There was not much else we could do, Ruth could not look for another hotel and we wanted to be near enough to find Eric later.

Actually the Arab hotel was very nice. It was several years older than the Swiss but clean and most adequate. We had lunch there. We sat beside a very green swimming pool and ate something very good, I remember. As we were going up the stairs I noticed a very old Englishman coming from a room behind the office. He told us "Good Day" and said something to the man with our luggage. I felt very much better to know that we were in the hands of a good English hotelkeeper.

Our room was lovely and it faced the pyramids and the sphinx. We were even closer to the sphinx than we were in the other hotel. We talked over our predicament. I decided Ruth was not too unhappy that we would now have to take a car and driver rather than that train that we had discussed before. I thought of the mobs of people and Ruth not too steady on her feet and decided we would have to do the easier way.

Eric had been sure that we should do that and so someone had to go and find the car and driver in Cairo. And that, of course would be me. street in Cairo

We had to get to the ship and there was no way to contact the captain to tell him where we were and find out how much time we had before the ship sailed. According to our schedule they were still in Alexandria so we would have to go there.

I had left my camera on the plane and I called the Swiss office in Cairo to ask about it. The girl there said she would call the airport to see if anyone had found it. I was to come to the Swiss office and she would know about it.

Eric took Mi Sang and me to the Swiss Air office and left us to find our way home later. Busses were good and ran often. He went to work and we went to see Cairo. Poor Ruth was in bed with her sore knee.

Yes, they had my camera at the airport but they would not be able to send it to the office downtown until there was a Swiss driver going. It would never arrive otherwise. That would be in about two hours.

I told them our problem and asked if they knew of a reliable company that I could visit. Yes, they did, and I could very easily find it, it was in the next block.

She came to the sidewalk and pointed it out to me, and suggested I come back in two hours for my camera. The Cairo Museum was close by and we could visit it after we had hired the car.

It was up a long dirty flight of stairs but at the top was a 'car for hire' office and they had what we needed. It would have been perfect for any Hitchcock Middle

Eastern movie, the men looked the part and the place was marvelous. We hired "Abdul," who would pick us up at the hotel and take us to Alexandria the next day. That meant we would not see much of Cairo, and Ruth would see practically nothing.

The night before Mi Sang and I had gone to the Cairo Bazaar with Eric. There was much walking Eric told us and so Ruth could not manage that. It was a marvelous, wonderful sight with all kinds of food, Arabic things of all kinds being made and sold and traded etc. It was a mad house but a controlled one. I was sorry Ruth had not been able to see it.

At the car rental the gentleman had pointed out the way to the Museum where, he assured her, Mi Sang would find lots of mummies. We went off and had a marvelous time, she in the mummy room, and me in the rest of the museum.

The mummy room had two entrances so that she could go past the mummies and then make the circle and see them all over again, again, again and again. I counted fifteen times while I waited. We then went to see the treasures from King Tut's Tomb. The best of the things were visiting London, so we saw the dregs, which looked pretty handsome to me. They could not hold a candle to the mummies so we didn't stay much longer.

We went back to the Swiss Air office and my camera was there.

I had tried to call the shipping office in Alexandria when we first got settled in the Arab hotel but the phones were all out of order. The Egyptian telephones were second cousins of the British phone company. When I was in Britain a few years earlier, a good rainstorm would put them completely out of order. Now this had been a flooding rain, and so, of course, no phones. Also I couldn't call Ruth to tell her why we were being so long, I was sure there were visions of abductions, murders and so on going through her mind. She had imagined everything! We were fine, we had a car and driver, we had my camera and we had seen many mummies and other lovely things in the Cairo museum.

Eric had been furious when he found out we had been sent off somewhere else. He made them tell him where we were and he came to take us back. We told him we were fine and it was all right. We rather enjoyed being in an Arab hotel. (Years later when Mi Sang had been "dragged" to a performance of Aida, she sat up from her boredom and announced loudly, "Mom, that is the scene from our hotel room in Cairo." And so it was, three hours later she announced, "Time does go by quickly when you are enjoying yourself!"

Eric was so good to us. I wanted to see the Coptic churches so badly and that was planned for the next evening.

Since Ruth could not do anything except stay in a hotel room it was silly to stay here since we had a wonderful set of rooms, SOMEWHERE.

Next morning we were picked up by Abdul, an elderly man, who turned out to be an excellent driver.

From Cairo to Alexandria July 27, 1978 (written on the ship)

The Mercedes arrived for us before 9:00. We were packed and all ready to go. The small boy of the hotel, Mi Sang's size, came struggling down the stairs with our heavy bags.

I hurried over with a tip for the lad and chided the man running the switch board for child abuse

We started off via the pyramids since I had had no camera when we were there before. I took pictures of the three pyramids and the sphinx. We went by the Jolieville hotel (our Arab one) and were soon out of Giza on our way to Alexandria. Immediately there were sand dunes. It was very picturesque with pyramids rising in the distance. These were other than the Giza ones, on the other side of the city.

Almost immediately we were in an Army zone. Evidently it was a training area, houses were being built. Our driver said nothing and we assumed he had been told not to. There were signs warning foreigners to keep to the main road.

Sometimes oases appeared that had small settlements, palm trees, other trees and some crops, but mainly it was sand. We began to see flocks of sheep lying in the shade. We stopped once so I could take a picture of a few goats being led by a Bedouin on a donkey. Ahead of that there were a few cows going into the village, also with a driver. Later we saw some camels in a similar herd but there were no more pictures suggested.

We went past a lake covered with brine that later would be salt. Small factories were there to refine the salt. The lake became a lovely rich purple color with many shades. There were figs growing all around this area.

Abdul had not been very active as a tour guide but he did tell us about the many monks who had found a place to live, pray and preach on this land some 2000 years ago. They had not done much and had had miserable living conditions in this kind of place. No water, nothing to eat and not much shade from the burning sun. Their followers had taken care of them, Abdul had growled.

By this time we were on the outskirts of Alexandria. Alexandria has only 2 million souls while Cairo at that time had 8 million. The traffic was not so frantic. Abdul took us to his company's branch office to find out where the shipping office would be. Some one led us there and I went in and was told the ship had sailed for Port Said and we would have to go there to get it.

Abdul was very angry that I would be so lax as not to find that out before we came here. I was getting tired of Abdul by this time and I told him I had no control over the inefficient Egyptian telephone system and I had TRIED to find out about the ship. The agent read our agreement with Abdul's office and thought we had paid to be taken back to Cairo if necessary, so that could be applied to taking us to

Port Said. It was a six hour ride to Port Said, so he was demanding more money. We understood that that was necessary, no one was arguing with him about that. We went to his office and they told us the amount of money we needed to add on to what we had paid, and they would let the Cairo office know what Abdul was doing (driving us to Port Said) not running off with the Mercedes. They then sent us to the best restaurant in town where we could all have to good meal before such a long trip.

Mi Sang had breaded fish with potatoes, Ruth had Spaghetti and I had rice with shrimp, Abdul had a nice big steak. We had beer and Mi Sang had a coke and I mercifully remembered her bottle of water.

By then Abdul felt better and he decided he could go on. More money, of course, but we had no choice.

Mi Sang had not eaten much of her dinner and I suggested she eat a little more. She just said, "Taste, it Mom." I did, and the potatoes were flavored with urine so I knew how they were fertilized. "Don't eat another bite," I told her.

Soon after we started on an experience of a lifetime. The drive through the Nile Delta would take us back some 2000 years in history. There were no roads, as such, just lanes and paths. We soon discovered that Abdul had no idea how to get to Port Said. He would stop and ask three people how to go to Port Said, or we supposed he asked that. If two agreed on a certain lane, we went that way. Very fast!

The women were washing clothes in the stream. They visited with their friends while they pounded the clothes with rocks. Mi Sang refused to look at any of these customs that we found so fascinating. Later we would wonder it that was the way it was done in Korea.

From the Delta of the Nile to Port Said July 27, 1978 Written on the ship.

We began our trip though the delta at 2:30, it would be a long drive. We had an excellent road to Tanta. We began to see the fellah in his field working with his donkey or oxen. Every few feet there would be a water wheel sometimes being turned by a blindfolded ox. The fields were small but had good looking crops in them. We saw wheat harvested, the rice a brilliant green, and cotton ready for the harvest.

The bananas, mango trees, and lovely old shade trees along the canals made a lovely sight for our mad dash through the countryside.

The canal was the water supply for the families. Baths were taken, water taken into the house for cooking, the family donkey would be bathed at the end of the day. I hoped he was cared for since he took much of the heavy labor of the family. Probably no more than the fellah himself, and certainly no more than the wife.

We saw an interesting family group, father, a long legged man rode the tiny donkey with the two boys of the group, mother walked behind the riders with three various sized containers on her head. It was obvious who was the beast of burden in that family!

Abdul, of course drove like every other Cairo Egyptian. He missed goats, donkeys, busses, cars and people, by inches while he leaned on the horn and roared on. They are marvelous drivers, they have to be to survive.

The houses on the way to Tanta were all made of mud brick. There were palm trees in each yard, goats in each doorway, and high mud stacks on each roof where pigeons lived. They obviously were part of the family's diet.

We turned off the main road to go to Kuba. Still we had cars, busses, donkeys of various size and many people. We roared on anyway and missed them all for some reason.

We passed some of the Egyptian boats on a canal near there – the giyasat – were looking like large, graceful butterflies waiting to fly on to some other spot.

The sun was going down and I wondered about the road on to Port Said, the road we were on was a very good one right on the edge of the water. There was almost no traffic by evening.

Suddenly we turned a corner and there was the city, with our ship right at our side. There was a body of water between us and the ship and we began to wonder how we could get to it.

By this time Abdul was our best friend and he said to leave it to him. He told us how much it would cost to take the water taxi. And we gave him the money to do the bargaining. In true Arab style it was done at top voice and it was hilarious, but we were glad we were not part of the scheme. Abdul had had a bad headache in Alexandria and we were afraid it would return with all this yelling and fist shaking. This is part of a true Arab's entertainment and Abdul was in his glory.

We finally got on their rickety little boat and started toward the freighter.

When we were almost there, they began asking for the fare, "We had not paid our FARES!"

They would take us no farther. "Yes they would, I told them and they knew very well Abdul had paid them, no, no, he had kept part of it. They screamed!

There was always that possibility but I really doubted it. We had trusted him and it had been fine.

Fortunately we were by this time at the ship and the men came to get \us, they knew these buggers very well.

They swarmed all over the ship but the ship's crew were also prepared for that. The cupboards were all locked and the hatches covered, there was no way they could find anything. So they decided it was time to whine about the American women who had not paid their money to ride in their lovely taxi. The Captain asked if we had paid them and of course we had and they knew it.

(pictures)Mi Sang in the captains's chair on the bridge of the Louise Lykes. Throwing the bottle into the ocean that the captain had fixed for her.

Some of the biggest sailors now appeared and helped them onto their taxi and offered to toss them into the bay if they didn't leave. We saw no more of them. Mi Sang was in the pantry making her first sandwich and finding a good cold coke. Ruth and I joined her and relished the good familiar food.

We were in Port Said for several more days but Ruth did not want to go ashore, possibly it was that taxi ride, so I never did get to see the marvelous Coptic churches.

As we were leaving Port Said, some time later, the Chief engineer, told us to be sure to note the "sunken ship" at the mouth of the harbor

Mi Sang's eyes were as big as saucers. I told him there were many things he could have said before he said that! Anyway I assured her that the war was all over now.

The next morning we were all called to the top deck to look for a ship that had sunk in the night. It most likely was only half way down, a real menace to all shipping.

It was foggy and that added to our uneasiness. Since we could not see our hand in front of our face there was not much way we could be very helpful. The one with the best eyesight had not been let in on the reason for this careful search. Soon we were told that we had received a message that it had been found, far from us and so all was well.

On our way back to Houston, somewhere in the middle of the Atlantic, we saw two ships being towed to Europe for repairs. Mi Sang wondered why one had such a funny color. No one could (or did) tell her that it had been burned, rather badly. The Captain then told Ruth and me never, under any circumstances, to travel on a ship with that registry, they were all the same and did not have proper maintenance. I never have.

We went to St. Louis and visited with Dwight, Sandy and Meredith. It was terribly hot weather so we stayed in their cool basement family room and soon went back to Honolulu. Ruth went to Parma, to have another year of school.

We went to Nuuanu School to find that Mi Sang would have that same teacher for her fifth grade school year. No one thought that was a good thing and so I began searching for a school where she would get some help

No school at the elementary level realized that children were coming to our islands from many countries not speaking English. It would be necessary to provide for them in some way. Had I known Maemae School was working on such a program for foreign children, it was just a little further down Nuuanu and I would have been able to drop her off on my way to school. I wonder now if that Nuuanu principal knew Maemae was offering that, and didn't tell me.

Someone suggested that a private school in Kailua would be a good place for her to go. They were able to give individualized attention to their students etc.etc. etc. I went to see the principal and liked her very much. What I didn't know was that they had some teachers very much like ours in Pearl Harbor and they would get their principal put out of her job the very next year. They were so busy doing that that NO student got much help, and Mi Sang got none.

These first year "know it all" teachers ruined two good schools and several children's education. Of course the ringleader was the whizbang that was to teach Mi Sang.

Without any help they sent her on to "Mid Pacific", a very college prep school who handed their new seventh graders a fistful of "Lessons". When they finished filling in all the blanks they would be "Educated". She was even more confused than ever and had learned nothing except to hate school.

Somewhere she heard that Hawaii School for Girls was the place for her. It was the social haven for the rich girls of Honolulu, never mind what they learned. I went to talk to the Principal: Same old garbage, "Our girls are considered individually so she will do well here." Little girl fun! Cinderella on Halloween, Ice Cream with Aunt Luree, Mi Sang with Bobby, our Cairn Terrier), Slumber party with her Nuuanu friends, Christmas, first with Erica, Santa at Ala Moana next year with Dwight and his family, Sleeping angels, Mi Sang, Diane and Meredith.

Serious things coming from the adoption hearing with Mr. Flynn, Violin lessons with Aunt Donna, Beach bums in St. Charles

Hawaii School for Girls It was so 'individual' that the science tests came from Iowa and were filled with information that they had not heard of from the teacher!

The next year she had the accident that kept her out of any school for almost the entire year. She had a marvelous tutor who taught her more than the other schools had taught her ever!

THE ACCIDENT

IT WAS A beautiful January morning. Mi Sang had rushed off to catch the bus for school. She was wearing her favorite cordorary aqua pants with the matching top. I supposed someone or something was special about the day. She was in a different school that seemed to be catering to the misfits, or lazy part of the kids being educated. She had been happier with it since Julie had joined the group and was more her type of friend.

Ruth our friend from Parma Ohio was still visiting us. She had been there for Christmas and had no reason to hurry back to the cold of Parma quite yet. She intended to leave at the end of the week.

I needed to get to school so I started off trying not to envy Ruth too much her ability to stay in bed and sleep. As I turned into Dowsett Avenue from Alika where we lived, I saw a crowd of people standing on the side of the big highway that went over the Pali. I went closer and say to my horror, I saw some one lying in the middle of the street wearing aqua pants and top. I must have stopped the car and I got out and ran to where I could see better, and of course it was Mi Sang.

A woman who had been sweeping up the fallen leaves was with her and she called to me that she had a gash on her head but it was not too bad. I saw that her leg was at an awkward angle and I knew there was much wrong.

We got to the hospital and I was not allowed in the emergency room and we were sent to a waiting room near by. The nurse came to tell me she was mostly upset that they were cutting her lovely pants off to get to her leg which had taken the brunt of the crash.

I was having chills in the waiting room and someone kind soul brought me a blanket to wrap around me,. A tall good looking man came into the room and announced he was the Best Orthopedic surgeon in Honolulu and he would be taking care of her. She had a badly broken leg but "it would be fine when he was through". Turned out he was right, she has a steel support in it but it works just fine.

Mi Sang was taken to the recovery room and I went with her. She was already asleep so I went next door to find Pastor Bob Fiske there, and Diane Matsuura, our church choir director. Several others from the church told me later that they had come to the hospital but could not find a place to park so they had to go back home. (They were my dear Japanese lady friends, and years before their husbands had taught them how to drive to their jobs, and to church and that was it. Parking had not been necessary.)

Ruth had called Cleveland to tell them that she would not be able to come home as she had planned and she would stay with us until spring so that I could continue to work. It was a good thing she did because there was no way I could NOT work since there would be some expenses that we had not expected. I appreciated her doing that. She was retired so she had no work to go back for and maybe having a little more time in Honolulu was not too much of a sacrifice. We both nearly starved to death since I would come to the hospital directly from school and then stay until 8:00 when we had to leave. When we did get home I was tired and there was nothing cooked, or even out of the freezer. We did go to restaurants and I wonder now why we didn't stay and eat at the hospital. It might have been closed by then. There were not many good eating places in that part of town.

Frank too ld me later that he had heard about the accident on the early morning news. and he cried, Mary Frances came out to see what was wrong. He called the hospital to find out about her. They came to see her later and I was very grateful for all the friends who came to our aid at that terrible time.

First the prognosis was six weeks in the hospital. Later this doctor said he had never said that and more likely it would be three weeks. That sounded better. 'so many people were concerned for us both. I had to go back to school as soon as Mi Sang was known to be recovering nicely.

The people at my school who had been ignoring me since they had gotten Mrs. Wakayama put into another school as principal and I had defended her right to ask them to make lesson plans for their classes, for goodness sake. Most of them were not doing so now that she was gone. Even they came to me to tell me how sorry they were. I was glad I could say she would be alright in time.

Mr. Oshiro, the principal at Pearl Harbor called me in to ask if this wasn't a good time for me to retire. I was 65 and could do so.(This would be all right with him, we were not friends!) There had been some other things that had been very difficult. A music teacher had been hired to handle the classes in the school that I had not time to teach. She had informed me that I was not capable of teaching the sixth grade classes, and so she would take them over.

After a few weeks with them and the other classes, she had rushed to a corner in my room with a pair of children's scissors and declared she intended to kill herself right there.! Few children happened to be in the room and none of them had heard her, I hoped, I sent a girl standing near me to get one of the counselors to come to my room as soon as she could. She was not trained in any way, but at least she would be able to take her away from my class.

The children asked me what was the matter with the music teacher. I said she had become ill and would be taken care of. One them said, "She is just nuts, that's all." I felt he had gotten it entirely right but we went on with our music lesson.

Later I was told that her husband had asked her for a divorce, I would understand that, too. Also those sixth graders that she knew how to teach and handle had refused to listen to her, they told her they wanted Miss McBride to come back to teach them she didn't know how to do it. They had met me on the play ground and asked why I had given them up. I told them I didn't have enough time and to be good and try to learn what she had for them.

One of the more out spoken boys, said, "She didn't know nothing." It was a bad time for her and for the rest of us. The children felt deserted and I felt badly for everybody. I had eight classes every day plus chorus twice a week and could not handle any more.

She was asked to leave and get medical help. A German teacher who all the kids feared was given my four classes of Sixth graders and they were made to use the time for a study hall.

I had loved teaching. When I first started to teach, I felt guilty at taking money to do something that I really loved to do. I got over that over the years, since it wasn't all that much money.

Mi Sang had been in the hospital for the three weeks just as the doctor had said, and during that time she had had the operation on her leg. On the day she was to have the operation, I knew Frank was not feeling well so when he came by I did not mention it.

Mi Sang happily told him as she shoveled down a very greasy Philipino stew. The doctor had come in earlier and I asked him if that was good idea since the operation was soon. He said he was not brave enough to take it away from her and he suggested I not risk it. She finished the whole thing and Frank understood what was needed, as always. When he heard what was about to happen, he took over. He entertained her as only he could and when they came for her he went with her down the hall until they took her into the operating room. She was laughing so hard she didn't even notice.

The nurse who had wheeled her down came back to ask Frank if he would take a job in the hospital. He had never seen child so relaxed. The doctor came to ask me what had happened.

The doctor came into the room to ask what on earth Frank had done for her Just entertained her, royally, I told him. He also asked if he would take a job in the hospital. I told him, no, he wasn't well himself. The doctor thought he was needed badly to help frightened children. I told him he had been with Big Brothers for years and had helped many children.

The doctor told me later it really helped her to be completely relaxed and ready for what was ahead. She didn't know that, of course, she just knew it had been much fun and she loved it. She was always glad to see him.

Poor Ruth had been with Mi Sang and MiSang had driven her crazy with some awful Rock music that she insisted on playing. She was in another room but Ruth was not happy. The school had a tutor for Mi Sang and she learned more from her than any other teacher she had ever had. She was also a nice person and could relate to her very well. She was in our Scottish group so we got to see her now and then there.

At Easter Ruth happily went back home and we got ready for Mi Sang's high school graduation. She was still on crutches and had been for some time Julie was kind enough to carry her books to the third floor where her classes were held. When Mi Sang went swinging across the stage to pick up her diploma, there was applause from all in the auditorium. There were many lovely leis and flowers of all kinds. It was an exciting evening.

Dwight and his family visit us in Honolulu,

I think we had discussed going on a cruise during the winter Ruth was with us. We flew to Acapulco to meet the ship. I remember seeing the brave young men diving from the rocks far above for coins that people would throw in the water below. The water was a beautiful turquoise color and there were many rocks below which they managed to avoid someway. It seemed a hard way to earn a living.

Cruise on the "Royal Princess) through the Pananma Canal with Ruth and Carolyn Boor.

We also visited some of the West Indies on that trip and went briefly to Venezuela.

The ship was very big and especially very wide and I wondered how that great bulk would squeeze through that small canal. When we were on the prow of the ship watching it happen, later in the week we wondered even more and it seemed to me it was somewhat nervously for all. The officers where leaning over the rail on the bridge watching the paint peel off in places. We did make it and it took ALL day to do it, We were under an awning supplied with much food and especially water since it was very hot.

It was a great experience. We crept thru cautiously and slowly. We made frequent trips to the bathroom and to the lounge to see what ever there was on for the day, we also attended the lecture and found out much about the building of the canal and the toll it took on human lives to get it done. I was pleased to see the canal begun by the French and abandoned because of the malaria.

Our staterooms were very nice. Ruth and I had a life boat to see around an over and under but we were glad they were on board and fortunately we did not have to use them.

Mi Sang was a little young for the cruise. We saw young men get down on the floor and look into her face which she was hiding from them. Carolyn was not so shy but there did not seem to be many unattached that were her age. I like being on any kind of ship so I was glad about that. The food was excellent but there was too much of it. We did our share of eating and enjoyed it all/

My reason for going was to be with my friends and Mi Sang and go through the canal. I really think a smaller ship might have been better, but seeing that behemoth grind itself through there was really exciting. Everyone obviously did their job well and there were no holes or too many scrapes and all was well. We got back home thinking it had been a good time.

MY favorite way of sailing is still and always will be the working ship, the freighter but alas, I can no longer go. That is one place where age makes a difference.

SCOTLAND

MI SANG'S EXPERIENCE with the schools had made her convinced that she was not able to learn at all. She was surprised to find herself on the Dean's list for her hard work in Early Childhood education courses in college in Pittsburgh. She had made A's on all her tests and papers.

She worked hard on her classes and her papers and it paid off.

Mi Sang made several trips to Scotland. We lived in many different apartments in different parts of the city. She took golf lessons one time and liked it except she had a hard time with the cute young redheaded teacher's accent. She told me she had no idea what he wanted her to do. She learned and should have kept it up when she got back. (20-21) flat in Scotland, street in Scotland.

Mi Sang is very athletically inclined. Everything she does she does well. One of her boy friends would not do anything with her since she always won. At last the Sports section of the paper is being utilized for more than wrapping the garbage!

We toured Scotland with several friends at different times. Aunt Genny Wakayama, Jack Wakayama, Donna De Neeve, Carolyn Boor, and Jean Hosokawa. I had taken my father when he was 78 with my brother Dwight, and friend Ruth Wetzell. I was amazed to find out how "Scottish" he really was, he loved everything about it except the coffee. He liked all my friends in Edinburgh and they liked him. My brother Bob had gone to school at the University in Edinburgh for one year after graduating form Harvard.

I went alone after I retired several times to work on some research for the books I hoped to write about Scottish history circa 1250-1300. I found some interesting material about the MacKenzie family (our cousins) and have written several books about that family. I bought a tiny apartment on Rutland Square in Edinburgh in 1988 and enjoyed it for several years as I did research in the Library in Edinburgh. Mi Sang joined me several times. One time she was caught in a blizzard in Ontario for several hours until the weather cleared and she could come on to Edinburgh.

CHINA

WHEN MI SANG was about fourteen we went to China. A young man in Honolulu had been working to become the company to take tours to China when it opened for tourists. (1981)

His father had been in China for some reason at the beginning of the civil war between Chang Kai Shek and Mao. He had needed to get with some group to get away and he joined Mao on his "Long March". America (Hawaii anyway) assumed that he was a Communist and put him in jail when he finally got back to Hawaii. He was not, he was an American caught in a bind. He was with all the potential leaders of the new China and later Roger was able to make good use of those friends.

We were one of his first groups and we were "trying out" new places to visit. We went to Urumchi and Turfan and the Silk Road, in Western China, as well as the usual places such as Tian, Lanzhou, Beijing, and we finished our tour in Shanghai.

I kept a diary for each day since we realized we were seeing new things. The Western Chinese were amazed at our faces and grinned at us through all the bus windows. It was a wonderful trip but we had all the annoyances that are present in a Communist country. (Too much attention at times,) a live-in National guide! food problems for some, we enjoyed most of it but we were used to Oriental food, incredibly unsafe planes and other modes of transportation.

THE CHINA EXPERIENCE
June 25 August 18, 1981

Tour by Roger Aryioshi Tours
Led by Roger Aryioshi

The big day finally arrived when we were to start our trip to China. Mi Sang and I got up early and said goodbye to our pets and we arrived at the Honolulu Airport at 8:00 ready to meet Donna de Neeve and the others of our tour group. We soon boarded JAL #077 for Osaka, Japan.

When we got on the plane we found only 50 passengers! This was unheard of in July, so we had all the room we could want for such a long trip. Our lunch was filet mignon with different Japanese delicacies of raw fish, rice balls etc. Little did we know that our next three trips via JAL would have the identical menu – and the last three were not very good at that.

We flew over French Frigate Shoals. This interested me greatly since when I went by freighter from San Francisco to Australia we carefully went by the shoals. It is very dangerous for ships and we went slowly and not too close to it. We saw it all on radar then. There was no danger to the ship since we have modern maps and the radar. We looked as much as we could through the clouds and it was interesting.

Later that day we flew over Midway Island. This was clear and beautiful. My pictures are lovely. I remembered listening to the news about it during World War II and how concerned we had been about it then. When I saw how small it was, I could see why it was a worry.

Osaka was hot and humid. We got through the lines for customs and immigration quickly and were soon out on the street walking to get on NO 6 bus to take us to our hotel for the night. We rode for an hour through heavy traffic and finally got to the terminal at the Dai-ichi Hotel. It is an interesting building. It is a round tower that shows up from bridges and planes often. It is brick red. Very tall and has a neon sign that circles its top. We were on the 19th floor in a very small room but adequate for the night.

We saw some of the "rooms" that Japanese businessmen use, they look like bunks with a TV and light, and are sandwiched in a pile. Not a thing I would feel comfortable in a country subjected to many earthquakes! I would hope they were cheap and easy to come by for a night.

We rested for a while, then we got up to see what was around the hotel. We found interesting little streets with many tea houses. They were (restored) we thought rather in the manner of "Ye Olde Japan" and so were quaint and charming.

The Japanese signs in neon were interesting and not as garish as they are in Hong Kong. Mi Sang convinced us she would starve in another minute or so, so we gave up our touring and went to the hotel to have our "tour" meal. It was another steak and quite good. We did not have the things that were advertised to be a part of our meal, but we had enough and it was good. We looked at the shops in the hotel. Things were not very interesting and very expensive. Perhaps it was the price that made me uninterested.

We really enjoyed our elegant bathroom. They were all one piece plastic and molded into the room. It was strange to stand by the washbasin and make a sudden move and have the bathtub shake! We were well aware we would not have it so good for the next three weeks. And we certainly didn't.

Mi Sang was deep into Television, Japanese or not, she understood she would have none for the next three weeks.

Next morning we were up early to see what we could find before time for the bus, but first came breakfast. The breakfast was excellent – juice, fruit, egg and ham, rolls, salad, pudding, sweet rolls; everything – we didn't eat it all but we sampled the unusual things for fun.

We found a subway entrance that was also the entrance to a shopping mall underground. I wondered about so much underground with the earthquakes so prevalent in Japan. Thousands of commuters were hustling off to their jobs. I wondered if we would ever get back to our right entrance and our hotel, there seemed to be hundreds of them. We wandered out near the American Express office and found a little temple. It was orderly, interesting and colorful. Many people stopped and said a prayer on their way to work.

We took many pictures and then got to our hotel and the bus to the Airport to get on with our journey. We thought we were leaving very early to get to the airport for a plane that would leave at noon. We did sit for quite a while. Mi Sang does not sit well and we had no money for a coke or anything. We were told not to get any Japanese money that the tour took care of everything, well, not quite and we could have used some money, we got along and Mi Sang survived. With all that time to spare, still there were too many gates, guards, we had no language; and so we gave up!

Beijing, China

The JAL plane that took us to Beijing from Osaka was a comfortable plane filled with Japanese business men or so they seemed.

We learned just HOW comfortable later when we were on the Russian built CAAC plane.

Our lunch was provided by Japan Airlines and it was the same menu that we had had the day before except this time the meat was very tough. Too bad to complain about filet mignon, but I think it was from goat!

We got very excited when we got closer to Beijing. Right next to the runway we were using (the other one was across the way!) were fields of excellent looking corn. We were to see that corn all across the country, and see it roasted on the streets but we never get to taste a bite! It was a gray, gloomy day but that only made the greens look more beautiful.

The airport was small but convenient. Our group of 18 fitted nicely in the waiting room while Roger took our passports and papers declaring we were NOT bringing gifts to anyone in China. No, of course not. Roger was, he was bringing books and had declared them. They wanted to see when he opened the box there on top was a tape recorder. This presented quite a few problems for Roger. (We were afraid we would never see Roger again!) He declared that he had not known it was there! His friend had done him no favor since he had had good relations with the officials up to this time. They took him away and detained him for some time, and I think kept the recorder. Soon it was settled and we were on the bus for our trip into Beijing.

We met our official guide then. He was a young man – Mr. Wong, I believe. At first, we didn't think much of him, and never did I believe him for a minute. He turned out to be very necessary for translation purposes. We teased him about not being able to believe him at all and left it at that. His attitude toward his own people bothered me considerably.

He was contemptuous of all places except Shang Hai, his hometown. It is more Western than we knew then, but we liked the Chinese part of the country best. What he did best was enjoy three meals a day and a nice bed and look down his long nose at the rest of us – Americans and Chinese.

We drove for miles on a wide boulevard with three kinds of trees on each side of the road. This is new for China since most of their trees had been used for fuel. Mao had insisted that they be planted and so they were. There had been a feeling that they had too many insects and "Spirits" that were bad for the people. Mao declared that this was not so and that millions of trees were to be planted. So, of course they were. The shade was much appreciated, and they were very beautiful. We also realized that the wonderful walls of Beijing were where that nice wide road was now.

All along the way there were police towers, not very tall but they made it possible to control the unbelievable traffic. The traffic consisted of many people walking, and a few horse drawn carts, and us. As we neared the city there were more busses. Some officious official cars roared by driven by army personnel.

We had passed a few farmhouses but not as many as we should have I felt, so then I knew the villages and farms around Beijing had been "cleared" to make way for the road from the airport to the city. So thousand year old city walls and homes were expendable.

Beijing was crowded and drab. One friend said that the person who got the paint concession in China would become an instant millionaire. We went by the entrance to the lovely "Temple of Heaven". Roger assured us we would return at another time. This was my main reason for visiting Beijing, the tiles in that building are incredible. The blue is not able to be captured by a camera, it is such an incredible cobalt, and the inside is a real "Chinese Red" also it does not show up well in photographs. I have seen many lovely buildings but I think that one is my favorite of all.

We did arrive at our hotel which was far from everything. We discovered that all hotels in China were built using the same blueprint. (This was true in 1981) No matter what city you were in you could go immediately to the dining room because they were all in the same part of the building. I followed that theme too absent-mindedly and almost went into the men's room because in the last hotel THAT had been the gift shop!

Our room was pleasant, the bathroom mostly worked, and the air conditioner was vainly trying. I had no quarrel with it, Beijing in June is ghastly hot, and nothing could get it cool. It is St. Louis or Kansas City at its worst with 9 million people added to it. We decided all 9 million of them walked the street all night long, or sat under the streetlight to read their paper. The babies were sweet little things and they were being pulled in Conestoga wagons. The wagon also took groceries or anything else the family felt it needed during the night. At that time there was only one child allowed per family and we noticed it was loved and cherished whenever we saw them. They were also diaperless so much dropped many places. I wanted a picture of the sweet little behind, but I think that was not possible. The mothers were very unhappy if they thought you were aiming a camera at them.

The prevailing wind brought strong odors of urine all through Beijing. The living conditions were deplorable. Many apartment buildings are being built and each family is allotted two rooms, strangely enough they are not happy. They would have much rather had their own ancient house repaired with their courtyard available on nights such as these.(or any other time) People are not considered in such a government so the "warehouses" were being built. We walked all around the neighborhood of our hotel and saw the picturesque warrens with a spigot nearby to get the water that you needed for the day.

Early in the morning all the elderly were out exercising. Tai chi, it was, and it was beautiful to watch from our hotel window. We learned later that they did not choose to come to exercise at that awful hour. (5:00 AM) They were cordially expected to be there, and attendance was taken.

Our first day we were taken on a tour to the summer Palace. This was where the Emperors and Empresses lived during the hot summer months in Beijing. It is not too old and the lake was man made and we were amused to see people "swimming" and then suddenly to see them stand in four feet of water. We were being drawn in elegant barges over the water. There were numerous Chinese style buildings. They were not livable, no place to put your feet up and relax. We did get to see the last Empress' bedroom, portrait and some handwork she had done. I had written a term paper about her in my Chinese history class in college. She was most interesting to me.

When trouble broke out with the Western powers, she was told that China needed a Navy in order to fight the "foreign Devils. She took the money appropriated for the Navy and built a marble "ship" for her lake. This was her answer to the needs of China. We climbed all over that boat.

We had lunch at the palace in one of its many rooms. It had been the theater but she decided it was not big enough so she built a three story one. We saw her bed where she sat and watched whatever amused her at the moment. There was a place where you could dress in Empress type clothes and have your picture taken. It was expensive, crowded and terribly busy so we passed it by. I would have liked to have dressed Mi Sang up and had her picture but we went on.

This tour had taken almost the entire day so we got back to the hotel tired and dusty. There was a ballet that evening and we all wanted to go. Tickets were obtained – it was included on our tour, we hurried dinner and got to the theater. As with everything in Beijing it was crowded

The ballet was "Swan Lake". The orchestra was ear splitting. For some reason it was amplified and all the F naturals instead of F sharps came blaring out. Poor Donna who is a violinist in the Honolulu Symphony was in pain and my ears ached. When the dancing started we forgot everything but that. I have never seen such exquisite dancing. We gathered that the Russians had started them off and they had continued beautifully. At intermission a vote was taken as to whether we should stay to see the rest or go back to the hotel. Some of us were livid, but too many of us were very old so we were to return to the hotel. We protested, we begged, we would get a taxi, nothing would do we had to go home. To this day I am sure Mr. Wong either did not LIKE ballet, or it was not up to Shanghai standards. Of course the orchestra was terrible but the dancing made one forget.

The next day we had an Appointment!, to visit Mao's tomb. I felt I would have gladly missed that and stayed at the ballet. However, we were hauled out and put in line at the appointed time. I must admit that it was very moving. The lines moved forward silently. We were ahead of the Chinese who must wait in line some times all day long. We were in fours and we divided when we got inside and went down each side of the crystal casket where he lies in state. He was wearing his simple Mao jacket and they told us he was not "keeping" very well. I was impressed. There is no doubt that he is revered in his own country, and they know what has gone on much more than I do. If he called for the Cultural Revolution, he has too much to answer for, if the orders were put in his mouth . . . . There is a large marble statue of Mao in the reception room before you go in to see his body. The statue reminds one of Lincoln's. We walked in Tiananmen Square and took pictures of the hundreds standing in line to get in to see him. Also of the reviewing stand that is located in this huge place. Then of each other to prove that we were really there. This was some time before the terrible massacre of students that took place in that square. They just wanted some freedom and that was not allowed in China.

I felt it was interesting that Chou en Lie requested that he be cremated and his ashes be spread in different parts of China.

There was a movement to do the same to him and have his statue somewhere in the square. His widow would not be moved and so it was done as he requested. It was much more appropriate to do it his way, I think, he was that kind of man.

We boarded the bus to be driven to the Forbidden City. It is right off the Square and would not have been available to the likes of us in olden days. Mi Sang would have been willing to pass by right then but we had to see the most famous, or infamous building in Beijing. There were first gates, second gates, third gates etc. all to protect the Royal family from their loving subjects. Our cute Beijing guide pointed out several charms that were on the way to the first palace that was supposed to keep the family safe. He grinned and said, "They didn't work!"

There was palace, after palace, after Palace – all dirty and unkempt. It would be impossible to keep them all neat and spic and span, but we thought no one had really tried at all.

Finally we got to the living quarters and it was most interesting. There were fabulous incense burners around each palace. They were made in the shape of dragons, interesting animals, big pots etc, These were so crowded that we had a hard time seeing what we wanted to see. There were mostly Chinese people visiting what they had been kept out of for hundreds of years.

Donna was lost and I was worried about her. This did not happen when Roger was with us, he was a marvelous shepherd and kept track of all of us, all of the time. She must have turned some corner to see something and we didn't realize it until she was not there. When we got to the bus, many palaces later, there she was. She had heard that we were to meet at the north gate so she kept on going until she got there and eventually we came long. She had met an interesting Chinese family so it turned out well.

We stopped at the Zoo to see the Pandas. One was a three month old baby and he performed like all other babies and was adorable. He played with his ball, rolled on his back, and ate his toes. His father and mother were in another compound and did not look as good as he did. They were to have an expert on Pandas arrive from America to help them with these pandas. I hope he came and could help.

I had to keep remembering that the Pandas were living better than most of the people.

We had an hour to pack and get ready to go to see the marvelous Temple of Heaven. It is the most beautiful building in Beijing, or almost anywhere else that I have ever seen. It was built in 1420 by the Ming dynasty and it is a hall of prayer for good harvest. It has no nails and is covered by the incredible cobalt blue tiles. No where else did we see that color. The inside has pillars that are each one tree painted in Chinese Red and gold. The inside roof is painted in wild colors but they seem right for the building. It is built on a white marble platform with a strange white marble fence around it. I could have spent hours in and around it just looking. We rushed on, of course, to another one a smaller version built by the Ching dynasty. They were smart enough to know they could not make a better one so they just copied it! This was the Imperial Vault – Altar of Heaven. There was a strange wall around it that would send an echo of your voice to anyone with his ear to the wall on the other side. We had great fun sending messages. Temple of Heaven

We had dinner at a strange new restaurant. It was on the third floor. We always ate on the 3rd floor. The ground floor was devoted to strange looking Chinese men usually, and noodles. We always had to drag Mi Sang past that floor. (It was the noodles not the men!) The second floor seemed to be Chinese families "out to dinner". So the foreigners were made to struggle to the top, or 3rd floor. The cleanliness of the place left much doubt in my mind. So I looked in the kitchen. NEVER DO THAT. There is nothing to drink in China except strange looking orange soda that was sickeningly sweet. I must admit I stuck to the beer. I always had tea for breakfast and for dinner if I had it all day long I would be having a nervous tic before evening from – too much caffeine. We judged each restaurant by the coldnes of its drinks. If we had water at any time it was served in a wine glass, WHEN we could get it

We went to the train station where we were to board our train for an overnight ride to Datong. We were early so we were invited to ride on their brand new subway. That was fun, crowded, but interesting. We could only ride 4 stops (that was all there was of it!) and then the bus picked us up and took us back to our train.

Getting through the station was a nerve wracking experience. One guide was ahead, one was behind us and poor Roger seemed to be running in between. Mi Sang had been told to watch what she was doing but she gave the impression that she wasn't. Roger and I both breathed easier when she actually was where we needed her to be, ON the train in this case. Donna tended to wander off and that drove us crazy too. She found herself without a seat or berth when the train had started. I have no idea what happened there. Mi Sang and I were in a room with another mother and her child, so no room for Donna. Lynn aged 17, and the only one on the trip near to Mi Sang in age, and her delightful mother. The girls had the upper bunks and they immediately climbed up into them.

The train was European vintage 1910 or there abouts and I loved it. No airconditioning, of course but with a fan in the room that stopped when you came to a station and really needed it. Since Donna was the only single member of our trip, she ended up with three men in a compartment. That kind of thing never bothered Donna so she got along fine. I go to sleep when I think of a train, I love riding them so much. This time in the middle of the night SOMEONE above me dropped a cup on tea on me. That ended my sleep but the cup wasn't too full so I didn't get too wet.

We were mostly sorry to be traveling through the countryside all night long and not able to see anything. We got off and into the very small bus that always awaited us. Datong is a coal and industrial town. The hotel was the same design as all the others so we felt right at home. Here the plumbing was out of control. There was two inches of water standing on the bathroom floor. It seemed to be clean water but still it was a little disconcerting. We went in only when it was necessary. To most people in China even a leaky bathroom would be as luxury beyond their wildest dreams.

We had breakfast and then went off to see the Yunkang Grotto. Thousands of Buddas were carved in the sandstone rocks and caves. Unfortunately many are deteriorating because of the soft stone. And the wind was very strong and since they are 1500 years old they are fragile. I took many pictures because they are unusual. Mi Sang had not had enough sleep and she was cranky and impossible. There was no reasoning with her at all.

We went back to the hotel after the tour and she slept for two hours then she was more agreeable. The bus ride to and from the caves was most interesting to me. We passed many carts hauling the coal from the mines. The roads were being built and were terrible. We drove gingerly on the riverbed at one point. The houses and people along the way were most interesting. I took pictures but the bouncing of the van and the dull day made it impossible to do well.

In the afternoon we visited two monasteries in the town itself. They were very old but well preserved. They had survived the Cultural Revolution because the townspeople had housed the young thugs there, thinking that they would not destroy their living quarters – or so the townsmen reasoned, and they didn't. It was a smart decision because they destroying most of the rest around the area. Datong Mi Sang at a jade screen

The following day we were given a choice, we could visit a pagoda and monastery that was built into a cliff and was six stories high up crumbly steps with no railings. That made my choice easy. Also it was $12.00 and I felt we had paid quite a bit and it might have been included. Donna and Mi Sang went and loved it. They are both part mountain goat, they also said the meal was worth $11.00!

The rest of us stayed in the hotel and several of the ladies hired a taxi and we went shopping. That was quite an experience. We were in new territory, these people had not seen many, if any, Americans.

As we were looking at the things to buy, the Chinese buyers would gather around us and they were smiling and greeting us and also pushing us into the counter. We would move back and it would start all over again. I bought a Mao jacket (Mao had the entire Chinese population in these for sometime). I liked the idea that this was not a "Friendship Store" (government controlled) There no one was one bit friendly and prices were high and quality low.

Crowds gathered whenever we appeared. Now I know how Elvis felt! Not once did I feel any hostility, they were just curious and friendly.

In every hotel there were two decanters, one filled with hot water, hot enough to make tea and it lasted all day long, the other had cold drinkable water. I bought one to keep water hot for $1.00.

The next day we reversed ourselves and returned to Beijing via the train. Some felt it was a hard trip with little to see. I thought it was very good and I had enjoyed it very much.

The Great Wall of China July 1981

One of the best things in China was the Great Wall. Parts of it had been reconstructed in the 1950's. The Chinese are as fascinated with the wall as are the visitors so it is well visited.

We had to start early, that had been the excuse for leaving the ballet in the middle of it. We had to drive 40 kilometers to reach the best place to visit it. The mountains were soon with us and I was surprised to see pieces of wall on many ridges. What good they would have been, I could not imagine. It was close enough to Beijing that I suspect when it was breached, it was terrible. The Manchus would be able to swarm all over the city in a hurry.

We all rushed out of the bus and started up the hill to the steps leading up to the wall. It was wide and not too steep this far. Lynn and Mi Sang ran like antelopes and were clear up to the first gatehouse before Donna and I got on the wall. We walked in opposite directions to see as much as we could. There were modern Chinese soldiers in one gate house and I thought it most appropriate, so I took their pictures there. They giggled and made faces and were glad to pose.

I bought a little jade duck at the concession stand. I wish I had bought more, it was the nicest carved jade that we saw. We were told that the government got rid of their jade carvers (killed them or made them do menial work) and we found nothing worth while for the rest of the trip. We had a rather miserable box lunch at the Wall. There was a camel there and we were told they were led along the wall at one time. It was a great day. Mi Sang voted that the high point of the trip. She and Lynn had been half way to Manchuria on the wall so it was fun for them.

We stopped to see the Ming tombs on our way back to Beijing. The royal Way had some delightful carved animals of all kinds along the roadside. We got to stop and get out and look closely at them to see how well done the carving was, Mi Sang climbed all over them and I took many pictures.

We rode farther and came to the usual "gate" behind which were the tombs. The grounds were dry and dusty but the trees were lovely. The heat had become almost unbearable. All around the Chinese were wetting handkerchiefs at spigots and wiping their faces.

We all went down into the tombs and found it cool and pleasant there. There were rooms before the place where the Emperor was placed with doors that fell shut to block anyone from entering. It seems that when it was finally opened – not too long ago, the place was a shambles. Evidently the last trusted servants had vented some anger against the body. Anyway, the doors were all properly shut and the mess was left – it is still there, so who knows?

We were ready to call it a day, but our Beijing guide had a sleeping Buddha that we must see. I had visions of another sleeping body but it was not to be.

This turned out to be a pleasant ride up a hill to more Chinese buildings. There were lotus pools and even they were UP – everything is UP in China.

Immediately behind them t be sure there was a reclining statue sleeping. We all said he looked as if he had been on a tour with our guide. Exhausted!

When we got to the bus our guide had Chinese popsickles for us. They were very sweet and vanilla but very welcome. Each area had its own guide. We found them so anxious to have us like what they were telling us and showing us. Whether or not Wong was a spy put there to see if we were entertained or not, we didn't know, but we found each one different according to his own personality. They all seemed to be interesting people. It took hard work to learn enough English to be able to explain something as complicated as Chinese history to a lot of difficult Americans.

Some of us could not hear because of age, some because we did not LISTEN, some because they were history morons and had no background or interest in something as interesting as this. The guides were never irritated (and we felt as if they should be at times.) I felt they had been very knowledgeable and interesting.

URUMCHI SINKIANG CHINA

August 1981

The Plane trip to Urumchi took me back to my early flights to Hawaii from the mainland U.S. It was a prop-plane and took many hours to fly the 2500 miles from Beijing to Urumchi.

We stopped for an hour at the Lanshou Airport, which was a new building, where the most interesting thing was the "john". The stench met one when the main door was opened into the waiting room.

One followed one's nose until you found the holes in the floor. How you managed that was up to your own ingenuity. American women are brave and able to handle most things so we all managed.

The plane was Russian built. We all decided that was how the Russians got back at the Chinese for throwing them out of China. There were no springs in the seats. We had been given seats in the first class section but Mi Sang and I did not make it that far. The rows were so close together that you literally sat with your knees in your face.

We met up with the very same plane in Tian to Shanghai, Mi Sang and I ran into first class this time and listened to the howls of complaints that came from behind us. That flight was only two hours rather than the seven hours we had endured. The First class was loud, roaring loud and there was nothing FIRST class about it, but we could sit on a seat and not on the floor as we had for those many hours to Urumchi.

Two hours out of Lanshou we came in sight of the Tien Shen Mountains which were snow capped and beautiful. This mountain range towers over the city and is 1900 kms.long, 4000 meters above sea level. This province has 13 minority groups, 12 million people (there are 9 million in Beijing) 5300 km border with the Soviet Union, India and Pakistan. There are many Muslim groups here, 9 of the 13 are Muslim. In Urumchi there are fertile fields which are irrigated. It has oil and gold, there are two deserts and the Sinkiang province has the second lowest place on earth – Turpan. It is also the hottest place in China – we can testify to that. Sinkiang has five months of real winter, five months of summer and two days of spring and two days of fall. It is a four night three day train trip to Beijing and a miserable 7 hour ride via the Russian Cargo plane

We did a little rushing and got to a Symphony concert. We GOT there at intermission this time so there was nothing to do but stay to the end! It was an excellent concert. The orchestra was as good as the ballet troop had been in Beijing, now if there was some way we could get the two together! It was Festival type concert with a conductor from Shanghai,(ah yes, only the best from Shanghai). The concert included Bach, Tschaikovsky, a lovely modern thing using Chinese melodies, a fine opera singer sang some Bizet, Rossini etc. it was all announced by a beautiful Chinese woman in Chinese. There was no such thing as a program and anyway, who could have read it!

The hall was packed. When it was all over we were the only ones who applauded. A friend told me later that during the Cultural Revolution they were forced to listen to all the propaganda crap and they sat on their hands and refused to clap, for good reason, it was terrible.

The lovely lady came out, looked at the crowd said nothing, then barked something in Chinese. The audience all jumped up and left, except us, we gathered ourselves together and went to our bus and on to the hotel.

We had been left standing there with our mouths open, when they are given an order . . . .

The next day we went high into the mountains to where the horseriding Kazaks live. We were to see some riding and visit a yurt. It seemed unlikely that they actually lived right there, it was too much of a stage setting but it was very interesting.

We had thought that Donna and Mi Sang would be able to ride but it just never worked out. The horses were on the wild side, it seemed to me, along with the men.

We were invited into the yurt. It is round, made of deerskin, had lovely carpets on the floor, and is very comfortable.

There was a very small five year old child, much spoiled who entertained us. They were all in costume and very colorful. We took many pictures.

The stove is a tin affair with a pipe that went thru the roof. The lady made some good food which we enjoyed.

We watched some skillful games on the horses – the women rode as well as the men.

The ride on up to a waterfall was beautiful, and COOL. First time we had been cool in China.

Next morning, Mi Sang did not feel well at all. She just wanted to stay in bed. It was too early for the elevator so we walked down 8 floors for breakfast before leaving for Turpan. It was evident that Mi Sang could not go. Several others were sick with colds and etc. Donna and Roger persuaded me that she could stay with Mary Ota and I could go on to Turpan. I hated to leave her but it did seem sort of silly to stay when there were several others there and Mr. Wong could take her to the doctor if that seemed necessary.

I missed her and wished she could be seeing what we were seeing, but it was a rough, hard trip and she was better off where she was.

The bus trip was long. It was mostly through desert. There were no restrooms so we stopped where there were trees and went into the underbrush.

Always the guides had melons so we were not thirsty. As we went down into the sink hole that was Turfan, it got hotter and hotter. When we got down they told us it was ten degrees cooler than it had been the day before. We went through a black canyon that was most impressive. When we came back the light had changed and it was not nearly so dramatic.

As we got nearer to Turfan we saw water running, coursing, through the desert. There had been heavy rain in the mountains and the water was clear down here. This month had been the worst in 70 years for flooding. Our bus crawled though some deep water with the roadbed uncertain, he went slowly and we were all right. He was a marvelous driver and took care to see that we were always safe.

We arrived at a Moorish looking hotel with a grape arbor in the middle of it. It looked and WAS cool. We sat down to more melon and Thompson seedless grapes that hung right over our heads. We picked and ate and ate. I am careful about raw food and especially fruit in foreign lands, but we got along fine with these lovely ones.

We had a nice lunch and then we all took donkey cart rides down to the middle of town, ending up at the market. The smell of different kinds of spices was overwhelming. We could not see how we could get any home with us, but I certainly wished I could.

The raisins are marvelous but the U.S. government will not allow them into the country.

Because it is so hot here, the irrigation water must be all put underground. The early people who lived here worked out an ingenious plan to keep the water from evaporating. They dug irrigation ditches that were connected by wells dug down from the top of the plain.

These were every few feet so it looked strange to see these pock marks on the surface of the ditch. The water was cool and plentiful. These ditches were built 2000 years ago and are still in use today.

Turfan is an oasis, of course and recently had many trees planted (at the suggestion of Mao, of course) because a sand storm a few years ago threatened to destroy the fields and homes, and it was decided to try this as a preventive measure. It is certainly beautiful – it is very green and much cooler than it is where there are no trees.

The flood some two weeks earlier had destroyed roads, a restaurant, bridges etc. so we had to go around. The guide told us 15 minutes of a heavy rainfall is a disaster. This oasis is 500 kms. below sea-level.

There had been a heavy rainstorm in the mountains and the water was running this far away. That month had been the worse in 70 years for flooding. The main crop was the grape and many vines had been destroyed.

The next day we got up early to drive over more desert – that was the route probably used by Marco Polo on his first trip to China. There were more washed out roads, we forded a small stream to get to Geo-chang, one of the early Chinese cities. It was flourishing probably 1 A.D. to 1500 A.D. It was a Moslem city, at least there are several mosques being restored. It was also near the only pass through the mountains, so it was on the famous Silk Route.

We walked all over it, it is likely three cities: the inner city, the outer city and the palace. It was also irrigated by the underground irrigation system.

Donna and I had slept badly. We found an inch or so of water under our beds. Not surprising. There were thin mattresses on top of hard boards. It is a new hotel and the bathrooms were just finished. It was also 495% better than anyone else in the town had, but it was hard on us sissies.

The next day we retraced our steps and went back to Urumchi. I was anxious about Mi Sang. She was better but still could not talk and her throat hurt. The next step would be to see the doctor. I had bronchitis, and Roger had not shaken his cold. He was the first one to get one in Beijing. Wong made an appointment for us and took us to the hospital where the office doctor's office was.

It was a big hospital and the doctor was a very nice man who had lived in Shanghai until he was "relocated" 20 years earlier. He had been educated in England and I think the U.S., his English was excellent. All those talents landed him here far from his family. They were not "allowed" to visit him and he had to work and could not get away. (Not allowed to go)

He told me Mi Sang had an infection of the larynx; He gave her medicine, some to take and lozenges to suck and told me that would clear in up in a day or so. It was quite common in the western part of China. Tiny particles of sand from the Gobi desert got into the throat and caused the trouble. You had no idea it was there. That worried me since the throat is often subject to cancer. He assured me it would clear up very soon, and it did.

Right after lunch we left for Lanzhou. We went back to our elderly plane but to better seats. We lumbered slowly along but actually arrived some 7 hours later. We then were told we had 1 1\2 hours of a bus ride. The hotel was a nice one so it was worth all the long ride and wait. We went through a canyon that had homes dug out of the sides of the mountains. There was a stable made the same way at many homes, Later we would see electric light coming from those man-made caves after night.

This was the most western hotel we had had so far. The rooms were comfortable, and the service excellent.

Roger knew the Lt. Governor of this province and that may have helped. We were to be invited to a banquet given by this gentleman later in the week. Roger's father had lived with this man on the Long March with Mao.

Mi Sang was still tired so we thought it might be better if she stayed in bed and did not go sightseeing.

We ended up at the Zoo and I was sorry she wasn't along. She had played cards with Linn so she was happy.

We went to Nine Springs Park which had been a Buddhist monastery. It wound up the mountainside. There are only steps going UP in China somehow I never remember coming down any. There were springs all along the walkway. It looked like someone had struck his rod and they appeared. The water was cool and made the walk comfortable.

The Zoo was very sad. The animals were all prisoners and hated it. The roofs were tile, old and beautiful. We went to see an old waterwheel which took water from the Yellow River and put it on the fields.

This was our day to visit a commune. We picked up the Chairman of the Commune and he told us about it while we ate our watermellon and drove to it. (We had our watermelon OUTside of the bus, so the juice would not fall in there.) Earlier they had told us Henry Wallace had introduced watermelons to China. Smart move, it was refreshing and not dangerous as water would have been. It was a fruit and vegetable commune and they supplied all of Lanzhou. 16,000 people lived on the commune. They were divided into 11 brigades, 82 production teams, everyone worked. The children were all in school. They produced 14,000 tons of vegetables, 16,000 tons of fruit. We visited a "typical worker's" home. Phooey. The furniture was the same as was in our hotel room. I took pictures, but I was not convinced.

Mi Sang was raring to go, she was getting bored with cards, I guess. We went to the White Pagoda Park in the afternoon. She and Donna climbed to the very top. I ran out of railing so I started back down. There were beautiful views of the river and Lanzhou.

We went to see some jade being carved. The experienced jade carvers had been killed during the Cultural Revolution so these were beginners. We saw very little nice jade in China. I bought Mi Sang one of their horses and it was nice but not great. It was very expensive and my little duck was much more delicate and beautiful.

That evening we had a reception with the Lt. Governor. It began with more melon and some tea. The melon was a little hard to eat with no plates, no knives or forks or napkins. He and Roger were exchanging compliments via Wong.

We soon retired to the dining room where there were three tables set. We ate with the hotel manager. We were amused (I was concerned) to find the Lt. Gov. coming over to touch glasses with Mi 'Sang's orange soda after every toast

We had fan shaped pupu's, jellyfish, sea cucumber, ham, beef, Duck-Lanzhou style, melon soup, cake and more, much more. It was very different from what we had eaten elsewhere.

We left after the banquet, after thanking the Lt. Gov. for such a lovely meal. The orange soda thing had bothered me a little when I remembered what Meg (my friend in Honolulu who had been born in China and had lived there until they had to leave)had said about taking Mi Sang to China at her age-14 I carefully pulled the dresser in front of our door and I was grateful that we left very early in the morning.

Every thing was fine and we left at 5:30 the next morning and got to the airport and onto the plane and I breathed a sigh of relief.

Meg had told me elderly Chinese men preferred their girls about age 14 and I should not take her there. Meg had been born in China and had lived there for several years, until the Boxer rebellion had forced her family to leave. Her father had worked as a principal in a school and his banked money is still there. There was no way he could get it out of a Communist country. I had remembered that as he made his way to her side for every toast. Fortunately, all was well.

Tian, China August 1981

We had arrived at the airport early for breakfast, and then we waited until 7:00 for our plane. I had not been too keen on breakfast, the remembrance of the stench that we had experienced before, I kept thinking about. We did not go into the main building this time.

There was a rainstorm coming as we ran for the plane. I was a bit taken back when I saw an old time prop plane the same size as the ones that used to go from New Philadelphia to Canton several years ago. Wong assured us it was a VIP plane, but it looked to me like it had been dug up from the bottom of some pile. Some Japanese business men – black suits, white shirts, what else? Got on with us and that filled the plane. They seemed a little surprised too. However, we reved up and it started off grandly and actually rose up into the air quite smartly.

We flew for some time, not very long, actually, and the landing gear came down and we made motion as if we were going to land. He circled the airport (it looked very small) and started down. Then it must have been the wrong one and he suddenly pulled the plane up and the landing gear went back in place and we took off in the opposite direction.

Everyone looked surprised and I looked at Wong in time to see him crossing himself! Then a few minutes later vapor came pouring from somewhere on each side of the plane. This was about the last straw, we actually had a stewardness on this gem and she came and said something to Wong. He announced loudly that there was nothing to worry about! Well, we were certainly glad to hear that!

Donna was sitting a few seats ahead of us and she said later that she wondered at that moment how she had gotten herself in this kind of a predicament. She also said she wished she were close enough to hold hands with us if worse came to worse. I glanced at Mi Sang and she was surprisingly calm until I realized she had no idea there might be something wrong. I saw no reason to tell her – yet. After all, Wong had told us all was well. Another half an hour went by, the vapor disappeared and we were circling somewhere else. I looked down to see a field of small bushes, some elderly planes sitting dejectedly around the perimeter of the place. There was some kind of run-way and we were aiming, it seemed at that. The rain was really coming down now and I kept hoping we would not skid, crash, and we didn't. It was a very bumpy landing but we were just glad to be down. Now what? The rain was teaming down and we were out with the elderly retired planes.

The stewardess came to tell us we were to get into a bus that we saw there. I could see that the windows were permanently down, and the tires were very flat. She came back to say no, we should wait that our bus would soon arrive. It did not come but a rattly old one did and we were to get into that. We were all so glad to get out of that plane that we rushed into the rain and dashed for it

It turned out we were on a military base! This! And because the rain was heavy our pilot had elected to come to this place which was familiar to him and land here. No doubt he had trained here during the Chinese-Russian war, Donna and I concluded. Why didn't SOMEBODY say so, give us some hope or something.

We bumped our way to some kind of waiting room and after 20 minutes or so our bus did come for us. We were so glad to see a familiar face. How the driver had known where we were, I will never know. So we were finally in Tian. This was the high point of our trip to China for most of us. We were about to see the famous underground army that was being dug out of the soil. Tian was one of the early capitals of China and there is so much history everywhere. Our guide was especially good here and we were glad that it was so. I was glad to see that Roger had gotten the color back into his face. Nothing ever throws him but that plane ride was too much even for him. Wong may walk home, where ever that is. (Of course, Shang Hai) This may be his last tour, and I could see why.

We came to the center of the city and made our way up to the third floor for lunch. We had to wait some time.

We found the facilities were over worked in every large city we visited. There were 2.8 million in Tian and only two hotels, and about three "good" restaurants. We could not get into a hotel in the "city" and had to go out into the country to a factory hotel for the night. It was a nice place I would have liked to have stayed there except that the food was terrible. It was not really bad but for some reason the kitchen staff could not get it together. Dinner was set at 6:30, we had arrived at 5:00. It was postponed until 7:00 and finally they fed us at 8:00. I didn't bother to go, I stayed in bed and tried to work on my cold. I felt stuffed anyway, we had great food and much of it at a normal time so one meal I could miss. They all came back to report that the food was wonderful, it was just hard to get it.

The Museum was wonderful. It was a series of pagodas with buildings going out from each filled with stales from ancient times and statues from more recent history.

Since this was the capital for several centuries, I was wondering if Confucius had been from here. I found his portrait on one stale. All this time the rain was pouring down and soon I realized that we were keeping those people sitting in the bus from getting to the hotel and the hot water that Roger assured us would be waiting for us. We had been riding in the rain all over Tian having things pointed out to us. The most startling was to learn that those small sized mountains that we had been seeing all around the town were man made and within each was the tomb of an emperor. They had all been raided long ago but the signs told who had been there and when he died and all. We had gone through flooded roads, several times the bus had almost stalled.

We drove for another hour and a half and found that the water was hot and lasted all evening that was a first for China and we were glad it was this night! We were cold and wet and happy to be in such a nice place for the night.

Next morning the sun was shining and breakfast was on the table in fairly good time and we were soon off for more visiting in Tian. Our first stop was Lady Yang's tomb. She had been a concubine to one of the Tang Emperors and very powerful in the country. She also was supposed to be the most beautiful woman in the country.

The Emperor must have been partial to huggable ladies, she looked as though she might have weighed 250 pounds. In an uprising she was taken away and killed. Somehow she rated a most imposing tomb. We could not go in because it opened later. We drove for many miles to the Tang tombs. They look like mountains and were showing for many miles. The road we traveled to get to them was part of the old Silk Road which started in Tian and probably ended in Venice. We had seen a part of it in Turfan when we were there. It seemed impossible that we were standing on some thing so important in history. All the silks and satins that Royalty wore in the Middle Ages (after the Crusades) had arrived by way of this route.

Always the tombs have a Royal way that have stone animals and warriors guarding the entrances. These were resplendent with Tang horses. The Gate to the tomb was a regiment of stone soldiers guarding the entrance. They had all lost their heads! Seems as though superstitious farmers had decided one year they were responsible for the crop failure, so they lopped all the heads off. Too bad, now they are protected, but it is too late.

Also at the entrance was a stele commenting on the virtues of the Emperor. On the other side was a completely blank one, the Empress had put it up for herself! She said she was so good and had done so much that there wasn't room, also everybody would remember what SHE had done.

The tombs on the hills had not been opened, but we visited others that had been. I liked the reproduced pictures on the wall. I took two pictures that turned out well.

It was interesting to see what kinds of figures were put into the tomb. They were mostly lovely delicate ladies dressed in what we presume were clothes of the time.

The famous Tang horses were being made in a factory near by. I bought one for Mi Sang. It was too big but all they had, so it did not make it home. I bought myself a small camel since it was camel power that took the silk from China to the ships of Venice then on to the Kings and Queens of Europe.

We had a long drive back to Tian, this time to the Friendship (Government?) Hotel which was right in the middle of town.

We were on the next to the top floor and the rooms were very nice. After dinner we went to the next floor up which was not a complete floor and it was just used for these performances.

The funniest performers were not on stage but were some loud Americans who elbowed their way to the front seats, made loud comments about what they didn't understand about the show and got up in the middle and shoved their way out. Real embarrassing clods! Thank goodness not from our tour. We saw one couple several times, acting the same way each time. Very embarrassing.

The performance was with stick puppets, the sound effects and music were great, The different characters seemed to speak in strange falsetto voices. It was obviously war scenes with the "Good guys" winning in the end. It was not too long and very much worth seeing.

The next day was the high point of the entire tour. We visited the Quin Shi Huang mau where the unearthed clay warriors and horses are life-size and life like. The excavation is in progress and we could watch the figures being chisled very carefully out of the rock like clay. We were amazed at the expressions on the warriors faces. Even the stance of the figure showed his personality, age, and military bearing. The horses had been pulling wooden chariots, and the marks of the wheels-long since gone – show on the earth. We walked all around the workingmen on a high platform above where the work was going on. When we first went into the building the light was just right to see the expressions on the faces. I couldn't stop looking at them. Roger walked with Mi Sang all around the place and explained it to her. She paid attention to him and I was grateful that he had done it for her. I wanted to buy a terracotta figure but the salesman discouraged me.

He said they were not well enough made to stand the trip home. I was glad later that I hadn't. I was able to get one in the Art Academy in Honolulu that had been better made.

We left there reluctantly, it was so wonderful and amazing. We saw the tomb from which this army was marching.

My notes from the terracotta figures say; we saw one old man, worn out from his army life, one rather pouchy one, one haole, several mongol faces, some smiling, mostly good honest emotions. It seems as if the soldiers were coerced into letting the artists use their faces for the figures. Likely it was frightening for the men to think of their faces being used that way. We walked around the working area and saw how the men were in pieces in the clay. It was a real job to carefully dig out all the pieces and assemble them. It seemed to be students that were doing it. I would have loved to have joined them. The soldiers were standing in battle rows. It was where the roof had burned and pushed them over that the greatest damage had been done. Otherwise it was remarkable how complete they were.

I was impressed at how calm and peaceful the faces were. There was no fear, there was some fatigue and some boredom but they looked like real people with real emotions.

I have always thought that when I hear THAT tomb is being opened, I will go and see what it contains.(If I have to be carried) Rumor has it that it is a complete replica of the palace with mercury for rivers, and all very beautiful. We were told that the artists who worked on it and were on the finishing touches as the Emperor was laid to rest, were killed as they came out of the tomb so that no one would know what was really there. They (the authorities) feel that it has not been entered and robbed as so many others have been.

Tian was the capital of China first 3000 years ago. There are tombs of Emperors everywhere. We counted six small hills that we passed without comment (six more tombs) We had visited so many that some of our tour members refused to go to see another one.

We went to Bampo village the next morning. It is 6000 years old, a Neolithic Society. We saw the excavation of the village. It was very well done and very interesting. We went to see the clay like yurt hut outside and that was where we smelled the musty, overpowering odor that must be in the houses where people are living NOW, that are being flooded. 80% of the people in one area of this province live in some kind of mud hut. They are not as bad as they sound. They are made from this claylike material that gets like stone but still . . . .

We stopped for a short visit at the Huaquin Hot Springs. We had hoped to go for a dip in the pool but we had to rush on to the city for lunch. We did see Lady Yang's bath tub – sort of big! Also we saw Chiang kai Shek's bedroom. It was very plain and as bleak as some of our's had been. The guide was happy to point out that he had had to run up the mountainside in his underwear when the Communists routed him out in the Tian incident. We saw high on the mountain a marble pavilon marking the spot where he was caught and we saw streams of people going there. He was let go after some bargaining. We all thought the meal could have waited while we went hot tubbing, but that was the way it was, we went on.

The meal from the day before needs some comment. It was to be a Szechuan meal – my favorite. I was looking forward to it immensely. Unfortunately the only seat left was one facing the kitchen. It was a very dark room with a huge coal stove in the middle. From there the chief cook presided with a ladle (big one) which she pointed and pounded and yelled her orders, or so we supposed. She was a young woman who obviously tasted her food often and enjoyed it. I went in to take a picture, it was something to see. On one side of the room there were fifteen or so people chopping, stuffing and rolling and making all those things I love. I did love them. Every now and then this lady would grab a shovel and put some coal in the stove. Someone was on the other side stirring something vigorously.

Cleanliness was not even considered. The dishes sat in the filthy sink, refrigeration was not in evidence. I went back to my seat declaring I would not touch a thing that came from that kitchen. Right then a big plate of the things I had seen being made on the side of the room was brought in and passed around. They were crisp and pipeing hot and smelled heavenly. Of course, I had two of everything. It was all delicious and not one of us got sick.

I got teased about my declaration. And it didn't mean a thing. It just proves that good hot grease can take care of anything. The last thing I saw in the kitchen was a big bucket of hot water that was brought in and thrown on the floor. It could certainly use it and that seemed to be the cleaning for the day. The dirty dishes were still in the sink.

We went to the Big Wild Goose Pagoda which is 1300 years old. It was built to house the Buddhist scriptures by the third Tang Emperor. The present pagoda is much bigger than the early one, it is now seven stories. Mi Sang went to the top. There have been seventy earthquakes since that early building and none of them has damaged the building

There were 300 monks in the Tang Era living there.

There was a rubbing of the man who had brought the scriptures from India to China, but I could not find a copy to buy.

Shang Hai, China August 1981

We had a miserable flight from Tian to Shang Hai via Russia's best plane.

Since I had learned my lesson earlier, Mi Sang and I ran like mad to get a seat in First Class. Evidently the Japanese businessmen had been on it too, they were all ready there. Our group then just got part of the first class seats. After all, First Class is not very big on any plane. We had a professor on our tour who was a bit impressed with himself, I was disgusted to find him there while his wife struggled with the uncomfortable seats in the back of the plane.

So the seats were better but the noise was deafening. It was only 2½ hours this time so it could have been worse.

We had a brand new Hino bus waiting for us along with some Eskimo Pies. It was still HOT so they were most welcome. We also had rooms in the Park Hotel. This is a delightful hotel built by the British. Not with the same blueprint that the other hotels had used.

The Kawashimas and the McBride party had the penthouse suite this time on the 17th floor. I liked this in Roger. Each two persons got a suite sometime or other. Other tour leaders I have been with have taken all luxuries for himself, I can see where that might be a good thing since he had business with tour leaders and others, but Roger never did that.

Unfortunately, we had a very short time in Shang Hai so we did not get to enjoy the luxury for long. After we got cleaned up and rested a little, we went to a French hotel for the best meal we had in China. It was a great experience, and the beer was icy!

We rushed off to an acrobatic show. It was long, and I might have been willing to quit at intermission but there was great variety and we even forgot the terribly hard seats for a while.

It ended with one man who was a magician who looked completely haole.(white) They assured me he was entirely Chinese but somewhere in his background I am sure there was an O'Railley, or some such.

His part lasted an hour but he was so good that we didn't mind, as tired as we were. All in all it had been a wonderful day.

We sat and talked about it all for a while in our luxurious suite but soon were glad enough to try out our very good beds.

We left the hotel early and went to a trade show. There we found many beautiful things. I bought some things that I had not been able to find earlier. Shang Hai is a good place to shop but I would have liked to have seen more of the city. Shang Hai is very Westernized. There is rather more crime in Shang Hai than where we had been earlier and we were warned to be careful with our purses etc.

We were back at our hotel for a very disappointing Western meal. We had hoped for some good Chinese food for a finish to our very good tour but it was not to be. I do have to remember our idea of very good Chinese food is based on Hawaiian, San Francisco, New York versions and they are much better than the real thing, strangely enough.

We were then off to the airport to take the JAL plane to Osaka. Donna was held up because of a knife that she had bought in 'Urumchi. She had no receipt for it. So the conclusion was that she was a dangerous woman. She was, but not that way! Roger finally was able to rescue her and they did find the receipt that proved she had bought it in Urumchi. I had a fold up knife in my bag and had had it for the entire trip and no one ever asked me about it. Several others had been caught with scissors etc. but I had escaped. It was a little fruit knife and so not at all dangerous.

The trip to Japan was uneventful except we flew over some beautiful islands with lovely coves, beaches and palm trees. We could not decide where they were. We had the same filet mignon lunch, still not very good, but we all ate every bite since we remembered how expensive our next meal in Osaka would be.

When we got off in Japan we put our extra bags and packages in storage. Donna found a locker but I put mine in bonded storage since I had not had anything to wrap them in. I got several large towels that I use for covers in the summer time. They are large enough to cover a single bed. I find them very comfortable and useful. I wish I could have brought more. They are not available that I can find here in the USA.

The other members of our tour were going on to Honolulu, we left them feeling we had shared something very special.

The Ishiis, the Kawashimas, Sue, and the Cohens were staying in Japan so we saw them briefly in the hotel later that evening. We were in the Toyo Hotel this time, nice enough but not worth the $70.00 we were paying per night. We stayed in and watched TV – it had been a long time for Mi Sang to be without it – she had really missed it. We took nice hot showers and got ready for the next part of our journey.

KOREA
AUGUST 14-18, 1981

AGAIN WE GOT on the airport bus to go to the Osaka airport to go to Pusan, Korea. There was no problem this time since we had only overnight bags – small airplane bags at that. Mi Sang had TWA, I had Knutsen and a New Zealand tour bag, neither of them very sturdy at this point. We had stored our big bags and a string bag with all the Chinese treasures at the airport the night before.

I had put ours in bonded storage. Donna had been smart and found a locker for hers. I wasn't sorry since we had not had a closed bag to put them all in, it was probably better to have them under some body's eye. It cost me $25.00 when I returned and Donna only a locker fee.

The flight was a very good and SHORT one. Donna laughed at the amount of garlic she found all around her. The way you can tell a Japanese businessman from a Korea businessman is by the amount of garlic is flowing around you. The Koreans reek of garlic.

The meal was the same thing we had had previously, dry sandwiches, orange juice and none of it very good. I will never travel JAL for their meals.

Mi Sang seemed a little uncertain about this trip to Korea. She had been having nightmares for years about coming to Korea and somehow losing me, and not being able to come home to Honolulu with me. That was one dragon I wanted to kill with this trip. Her face was a little serious when we got into the terminal.

In the small terminal several Koreans spoke but she did not look their way at all. I told them she was an American and did not understand a word. They were mainly curious about her because she did not look at all like the little orphan girl who came to me earlier. However, she certainly did look Oriental so they were confused.

At the tourist desk in Pusan a man found us a hotel near to the railway station. We intended to take the train to Seoul the next day and it would help to be close to the train. After a long ride into the city, we were let off near to the hotel. It was very comfortable and we were close to the station. By this time money was getting to be a problem. Donna was very low and so were we.

We paid for our rail tickets and I hoped the "Compassion" Office would cash some checks for me the next day. The hotel would take our credit cards and we had our plane tickets, However this was Friday and we had to get through the week-end. I bought some fruit for breakfast and I saw some shell fish and I was eager to try them somewhere. We smelled a good bakery and got some good things there.

I thought the hotel dining room was too expensive for us and we looked around the area and found a small restaurant and Donna liked the smell coming from it. We saw woks on gas rings on the tables and the condiments that went along with it looked wonderful.

We decided we wanted to try it and the next step was to try to find out the price. That was hilarious since it was all in sign language. We waited impatiently for the feast and a feast it was! There was some of the shell fish that I had longed for with a great kim chee sauce. Mi Sang remembered some of the things we were eating with great delight. The price turned out to be what we hoped it might be, $4.00 each, and worth every penny

The next day was Saturday and a Korean holiday. Donna had a good idea that we should go to a park on the other side of town and see what was there. It was a great idea but we did have tickets on the Blue train to Seoul and that was at 1:00PM and we would not dare to miss the train.

We got off the bus downtown and a nice young man LED us several blocks to where the bus for the park departed. We got on it and enjoyed watching the people on the streets as we were on our way to the park. Mi Sang found some dried fish that were being toasted on a charcoal burner and she remembered them from her childhood. We got one and then several more and Donna and I found we liked them too.

We walked a bit in the park, we had taken the wrong way to be able to see the shoreline and the pinnacle but it was beautiful any way.

We rode the bus around the park and then hightailed it to our hotel to pick up our things and get ready to board the train.

We gave in and got a bowl of soup at the hotel, it was very good. And we needed to get to the station to stand in line. Yes, we had tickets and a reserved seat but this was a holiday and people always hoped in such a situation that someone would not show and they would be able to get a seat.

The Blue train is a very fast, clean super train that goes from Pusan to Seoul in a little over 5 hours. We were put in the wrong car at first and so we had to fuss around and get that sorted out. Perhaps it was a bad thing that we did. For the next five hours we were annoyed by some naughty little Korean boys.

The people in our car were the upper crust of society and their children EXPRESSED themselves, but I really think it was because the child's mother was too cheap to get her son a seat. So she sat and slept while he got tired and cranky. Finally I held him on my lap for two hours and he slept very well. No little boy can run up and down the aisles and throw garbage on people for three hours and not get into trouble.

"THE ROYAL PRINCESS"
AND THE PANAMA CANAL

M I SANG AND I came from Honolulu, Carolyn Boor and Ruth Wetzell met us in Los Angeles and we boarded the Princess Line ship, "The Royal Princess" for a trip through the Panama Canal.

The Canal was to be turned over to the Chinese for some strange reason in 1999. We wanted to be on while it was being manned by the U.S. since that ship was enormous and we wondered how it would make it through that narrow passage.

First we stopped at Acapulco, (Mexico) And I must confess that all I remember was watching the boy jumping from the cliff to the ocean below for change that followed him down. He made it gracefully and safely and I will never know how he did it. The rocks were sharp and numerous and evil looking but he got up and scurried up to do it again.

The food on the Princess lines was very good, not as elegant as on the QE2, but too much of it and we ate generously.

We had to wait while another ship went through the canal. It was marvelous to see how it all worked out, and how carefully and deftly everything worked to get the ship positioned ready to slip right though to the body of water that went out to the Atlantic ocean.

When it was our ship's turn to go, we had found a spot that would allow us to see all the activity of the day (and a day it would take us) and still allow us to come and go as we pleased. Of course everyone had the same idea, so it was a very crowded deck. That big ship went very carefully with the officers hanging over the bridge to be sure not too much paint was lost. As we got nearer to the other side I was interested to see the original "ditch" that had been dug by the French. They had not gone very far when the mosquito carrying malaria wiped out their workers and stopped that effort. I understand the newspapers in the American cities declared that it would never be done. Quinine came along and was found to defeat malaria and so it started being considered once again. It was a formidable task, and it took some time but it was successful.

Our trip through the canal was quite an experience and I enjoyed it. We had very red faces and noses but we had been sheltered somewhat so it soon went away.

We looked forward to our introduction to South America, at Caracas, Venezuela. The long bay taking us to the city was most interesting. There were many small islands with palm trees and beautiful beaches before we got to the city. We rushed around seeing as much as we could. I succumbed to a small emerald; it was so small I can still hardly find it! Silly!

Our next stop was Aruba. The trees fascinated me, they were not very tall and the tops all pointed the same way! The winds were very strong and came from the same direction all the time. So the trees were permanently disfigured.

We lived on the ship, of course, so we went off to see what was offered and came home to eat.

We visited Antigua. I loved the steel bands and there was a great one there that greeted us at the dock. I think the "party" (ours) went to the beach that day. The beaches were all glorious, white sand ones that went on for miles. We had a look out that we went to see, English Bay. (not sure of the name) It was easy to imagine ships of the 16th century there with billowing sails and handsome English men manning the ships.

We went to Martinique. This was interesting because of its French influence. The volcano Mt. Pele was looming over us as we went up into the mountains for a fancy lunch. We stopped at the village where the black man had been in the jail during the eruption and had survived. Only person who did in any of the villages that was in the way of the lava.

We moved on to St. Thomas and St. John. There were supposed to be big bargains there from some boutiques in Europe. We did have some good tours that took us to out of the way beaches. These are U.S. Possessions and so have all the problems that we suffer; Traffic, high prices, crime and all the other things that civilization seems to bring. They are very beautiful islands.

Our last island was Porto Rico and that was only to dash from the ship to the airport.

Our plane was American and an old one. The pilot seemed to be unsure of his route. Mi Sang and I were to go to St. Louis and spend a few days with Dwight and family. First of all we smelled electric wires smoldering. Then he got down lower and lower, and we went slower and slower. I was very glad when he found the right place and we deliberately landed. I was glad the landing came before the wires really caused some trouble.

Our trip home was uneventful and we were delighted to get home to our furry family and to find they were all right and glad to see us.

Ruth and Carolyn got home safely and went back to work. It had been a different kind of trip and interesting.

A WORKING TOUR WITH KOALAS IN AUSTRALIA FOR MI SANG

Eilean Donan Castle

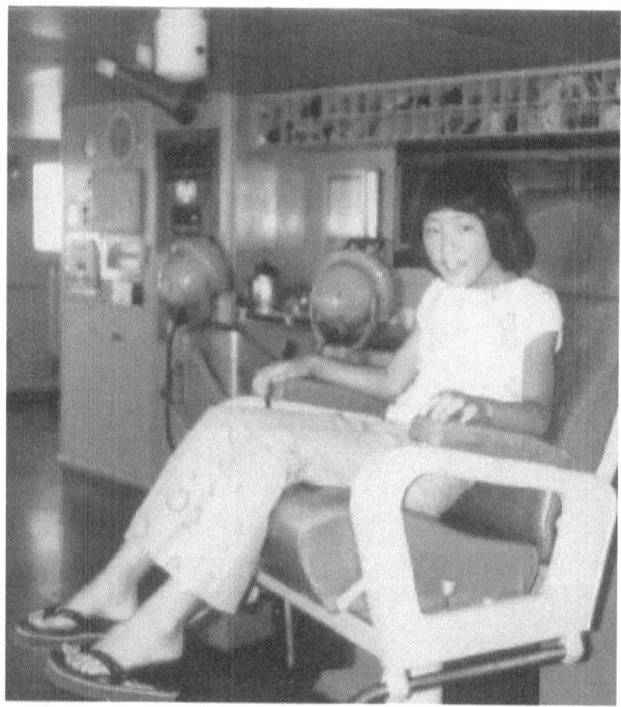

Mi Sang in "Ms. Master's Chair" on the Freighter

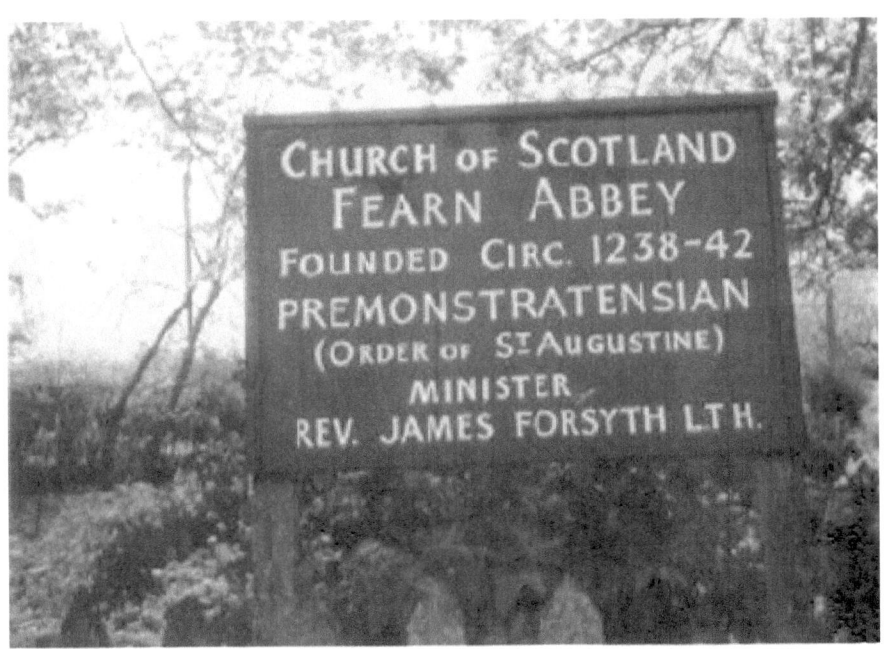

Bottle overboard from the Freighter

At the war memorial in Edinburgh

5 Sisters of Kintail, Scotland

www.ingramcontent.com/pod-product-compliance
Lightning Source LLC
Chambersburg PA
CBHW021241280526
45784CB00005B/2196